WISDOM LITERATURE

General Editors
Core Biblical Studies
Louis Stulman, *Old Testament*
Warren Carter, *New Testament*

Other Books in the Core Biblical Studies Series
The Apocrypha by David A. deSilva
The Dead Sea Scrolls by Peter Flint
Apocalyptic Literature in the New Testament by Greg Carey
God in the New Testament by Warren Carter
Christology in the New Testament by David L. Bartlett
John and the Johannine Letters by Colleen M. Conway
The Holy Spirit in the New Testament by John T. Carroll

CCORE BIBLICAL STUDIES

WISDOM LITERATURE

SAMUEL E. BALENTINE

Abingdon Press

Nashville

WISDOM LITERATURE

Copyright © 2018 by Abingdon Press

This book is printed on acid-free paper.

Library of Congress Cataloging-in-Publication Data has been requested.

ISBN 978-1-4267-6502-5

18 19 20 21 22 23 24 25 26 27—10 9 8 7 6 5 4 3 2 1
MANUFACTURED IN THE UNITED STATES OF AMERICA

For Eleanor, Tenley, and Grayson
through whom I can imagine
all the wonders that will be

Contents

General Preface

"All beginnings are hard," muses David Lurie in Chaim Potok's novel *In the Beginning*. "The midrash says, 'All beginnings are hard.' You cannot swallow all the world at one time." Whether learning to ride a bike or play an instrument, starting a new job, or embarking on a course of study, beginnings bristle with challenges and opportunities. The Core Biblical Studies series (CBS) is designed as a starting point for those engaged in Old Testament study. Its brief though substantive volumes are user-friendly introductions to core subjects and themes in biblical studies. Each book in the series helps students navigate the complex terrain of historical, social, literary, and theological issues and methods that are central to the Old Testament.

One of the distinctive contributions of CBS is its underlying commitment to bring together our most respected scholars/teachers with students in the early stages of their learning. As we noted in our first book in the series, "Drawing on the best scholarship, written with the need of students in mind, and addressed to learners in a variety of contexts, these books will provide foundational concepts and contextualized information for those who wish to acquaint themselves . . . with a broad scope of issues, perspectives, trends, and subject matter in key areas of interest."

One might think that such an arrangement is commonplace, but this is not always the case. Take, for example, introductory classes at many of our largest universities. Rarely are 101 classes taught by our most experienced instructors. This standard practice is in part a cost-saving measure, but at the same time it misses a unique opportunity. CBS addresses this common oversight by entrusting students' beginnings to mentors who will prepare them for subsequent inquiry.

The books in this series not only serve to introduce beginners to biblical texts but also aim to meet the needs of teachers who are well aware of the complexities of interpreting meaning. The process of meaning making of Old Testament texts is framed and influenced by a range of factors including the workings behind the text (diachronic), within the text (synchronic), and after the text by subsequent reading communities (the so-called Nachleben). This dynamic process is refracted through the lens of scholarly methodologies as well as the social location of the reader. No text is an island, and no interpreter stands outside of his or her own particular time and place. An understanding of this amalgam, especially the diversity of interpretive approaches, is rich with possibilities and crucial to informed readings; but at the same time, it can be almost unwieldy in light of time constraints and other limitations. CBS volumes seek to help teachers navigate this complicated terrain in the classroom and so are "unapologetically pedagogical."

The goal of each volume is to help readers encounter the biblical text for themselves and become more informed interpreters, and to set them on a joy-filled trajectory of life-long learning.

Louis Stulman

General Editor

Abbreviations

General abbreviations

BCE .... before the common era

ca. .... *circa* = about, approximately

CE .... common era

cf. .... *confer* = compare

ch(s) .... chapter(s)

ed(s) .... editor(s), edited by, edition

e.g .... *exempli gratia* = for example

esp .... especially

Heb .... Hebrew (text)

ibid .... *ibidem* = in the same place

i.e .... *id est* = that is

ll .... lines

repr .... reprint(ed)

trans .... translated by

v(v) .... verse(s)

vol(s) .... volume(s)

YHWH .... Hebrew (consonantal) letters signifying the divine name

Abbreviations of biblical books and other ancient writings

Gen .... Genesis

Exod .... Exodus

Lev .... Leviticus

Num .... Numbers

Deut................................ Deuteronomy

Judg .... Judges

1–2 Sam.......................... 1–2 Samuel

1–2 Kgs........................... 1–2 Kings

Neh................................. Nehemiah

Ps(s) .... Psalm(s)

Prov................................ Proverbs

Eccl .... Ecclesiastes

Song............................... Song of Solomon

Isa .... Isaiah

Jer .... Jeremiah

Lam................................ Lamentations

Ezek .... Ezekiel

Dan................................ Daniel

Hos .... Hosea

Mic .... Micah

Nah................................ Nahum

Hab................................ Habbakuk

Zech............................... Zechariah

Bar .... Baruch

Sir .... Sirach (Ecclesiasticus)

Wis .... Wisdom of Solomon

LXX .... Septuagint (Old Greek translation of the Old Testament)

Abbreviations of modern publications

AB................................. Anchor Bible and Yale Anchor Bible

AnBib............................. Analecta biblica

BJS................................ Brown Judaic Studies

BZAW	Beihefte zur Zeitschrift für die alttestamentliche Wissenschaft
CEB	Common English Bible
HTR	Harvard Theological Review
HUCA	Hebrew Union College Annual
JBL	Journal of Biblical Literature
JSJSup	Journal for the Study of Judaism, Supplement Series
JSOT	Journal for the Study of the Old Testament
JSOTSup	Journal for Study of the Old Testament, Supplement Series
LHBOTS	The Library of Hebrew Bible/Old Testament Studies
NAB	New American Bible
NEB	New English Bible
NIB	New International Bible
NIV	New International Version (of the Bible)
NKJV	New Kings James Version (of the Bible)
NJPS	New Jewish Publication Society (Tanakh)
NRSV	New Revised Standard Version (of the Bible)
NTS	New Testament Studies
OTL	Old Testament Library
REB	Revised English Bible
VT	Vetus Testamentum
WBC	Word Bible Commentary
ZAW	Zeitschrift für die alttestamentiche Wissenschaft

Introduction
Wisdom and *wisdom*

"To some degree, the natural history of wisdom can be seen as a never-ending battle between the forces of theology and those of secularization, between a top-down, benevolent, dispensed, and divine form of wisdom and a bottom-up, organic, hard-earned human form of wisdom. Put simply, is wisdom a human quality, achieved by human intelligence and insight? Or is wisdom a heavenly gift, bestowed by the gods (or God), utterly inaccessible to mortals who do not subscribe to one or another of the world's religions? This question was embedded in the earliest versions of the Hebrew Bible, in Eve's apple and Solomon's dream. . . . In such a setting, Wisdom (with a capital *W*) comes from on high, and wisdom (with a small *w*) contracts to the rather more modest spheres of familial and communal enterprise."[1]

The beginning of Wisdom (with a capital *W*) in ancient Israel has traditionally been traced to Solomon. Faced with the task of governing Israel, Solomon prayed for a "discerning mind . . . to distinguish good from evil" (*lēb šōmēaʿ . . . lĕhābîn bēn ṭôb lĕrāʿ*, 1 Kgs 3:9). It pleased God that Solomon did not ask for long life, wealth, and victory over his enemies— the practical benefits typically associated with human wisdom (with a small *w*; e.g., Prov 3:13-17)—and so God doubled Solomon's blessing by giving him not only "a wise and understanding mind" (*lēb ḥākām wĕnābôn*) but also the riches of life he did not request (1 Kgs 3:12-14). Solomon exemplifies the piety that recognizes wisdom is a gift from God, not a human achievement. This truth crystalizes in the maxim that introduces the

1

book of Proverbs, the Old Testament book most closely associated with the lore of Solomon's wisdom: "Wisdom begins with the fear of the Lord" (Prov 1:7).

As Stephen Hall recognizes, however, the search for Wisdom or wisdom to distinguish between good and evil does not begin with God's answer to Solomon's prayer. It begins—and perhaps could have ended—with God's proscription to Adam and Eve: "Don't eat from the tree of knowledge of good and evil [*da'at ṭôb wārā'*], because on the day you eat from it, you will die" (Gen 2:17). The primordial narrative places the temptation to go beyond God's prohibition on the forked tongue of the serpent, "the most intelligent[2] of all the wild animals that the Lord God had made" (Gen 3:1). The interchange between the serpent and the woman has been described as the "Garden of Eden moment" in human evolution, the moment when curiosity triggers a step across a forbidden threshold of knowledge into a "cognitive world of moral choice."[3]

> [The serpent] said to the woman, "Did God really say that you shouldn't eat from any tree in the garden?"
>
> The woman said to the snake, "We may eat the fruit of the garden's trees but not the fruit of the tree in the middle of the garden. God said, 'Don't eat from it, and don't touch it, or you will die.'"
>
> The snake said to the woman, "You won't die! God knows that on the day you eat from it, you will see clearly and you will be like God, knowing good and evil [*yōdě'ê ṭôb wārā'*]." The woman saw that the tree was beautiful with delicious food and that the tree would provide wisdom [*lěhaśkîl*], so she took some of its fruit and ate it, and also gave some to her husband, who was with her, and he ate it. Then they both saw clearly and knew that they were naked. (Gen 3:1-7)

The account merits close scrutiny at many levels, but its fundamental thrust is reasonably clear. Some fruit, that is, some knowledge, is available and accessible to human beings, but other fruit, here specified as the "knowledge of good and evil," is by divine decree inaccessible and forbidden. The woman transgresses this decree with an act of autonomous reasoning. She looks, she sees, she thinks, and she decides. To gain insight (*śekel*; CEB, "wisdom") into life in the garden, she reaches for more than she can grasp. Were Eve one of Plato's students, she would have been commended for her aspirations.

> If a man has seriously devoted himself to the love of learning and to true wisdom, if he has exercised these aspects of himself above all, then there is absolutely no way that his thoughts can fail to be both immortal and divine, should truth come within his grasp.[4]

Eve's education takes place in God's garden, however, not in Plato's academy. According to the Hebrew Bible's account of the genesis of wisdom, the woman and the man, primordial progenitors of *Homo sapiens* ("wise persons") are cursed not commended. They are sent into exile east of Eden, their (and our) access to the Tree of Life forever blocked by the flaming swords of God's protective cherubim (Gen 3:24). Refusing to accept the boundary between Wisdom and *wisdom* becomes in effect the original sin.[5]

These two biblical figures, Solomon and Eve, are paradigms for an introduction to the wisdom tradition in ancient Israel. God both grants wisdom and forbids it. The human quest for wisdom is primordial but not always blessed, insatiable but never satisfied. I suppose that readers of a book like this are pursuing their own questions about knowledge and wisdom, looking both to and beyond the biblical text for elusive answers. Does the Old Testament privilege one model over the other? Is Solomon-like piety the route to wisdom? Is Eve-like audacity a sure ticket to exile?

As one might expect of any search for the source of wisdom, no answer proposed to either of these questions is unarguable. Of the five wisdom books surveyed here, three (Proverbs, Sirach, and Wisdom of Solomon) agree that piety (the "fear of the Lord") is the beginning of wisdom; two (Job and Ecclesiastes) contest this affirmation and probe, against all caution, other perspectives. On the one hand, one may argue that a rough chronological ordering of the five books suggests a hermeneutical frame for interpreting the whole, beginning (Proverbs) and ending (Sirach and Wisdom of Solomon) with the Solomonic model of piety. On the other hand, we might read the two books located inside this frame, Job and

Ecclesiastes, as dissonant voices that resist conformity to what is expected or required of those who search for wisdom, thus denying the frame any claim to authority. Like Eve, Job and Qohelet cross boundaries and violate norms, and perhaps, like Eve, the wisdom tradition sought to banish or marginalize them. Job's friends rebuke him.[6] Qohelet's epilogist corrects him (Eccl 12:13-14). Or, perhaps it was the wisdom tradition itself that insisted their voices not be erased from the record; they may be muted, but they are not silenced.

Whatever internal tensions these books may reflect, and whatever perspectives may have ultimately gained majority support among the sages, we may wonder if the wisdom tradition in its entirety was anything more than a minor voice in ancient Israel. The collection of wisdom books is certainly substantial and can be extended still further to include texts not covered here, for example, wisdom psalms (e.g., Psalms 1, 37, 73, 91, 119, 128) and sapiential texts found among the Dead Sea Scrolls (e.g., 4QInstruction).[7] Nevertheless, previous generations of biblical scholars largely viewed wisdom as an alien resident within the Hebrew Bible. Proverbs, Job, and Ecclesiastes give little or no attention to covenant and law, revelation, and divine providence. Their "humanistic" perspective seemed to many to be more consonant with Greek philosophy than with what was assumed to be the normative ideas rooted in the historical and prophetic books of the Old Testament. Indeed, we may suspect that over time the sages themselves recognized the problem. Sirach constructs the missing bridge between wisdom and covenantal obedience: "Fearing the Lord is the whole of wisdom, and all wisdom involves doing the Law" (Sir 19:20; cf. 1:16; 21:11; 23:27). The Wisdom of Solomon assigns God's providential role in history to Wisdom (Wis 10–22). In recent years, biblical scholars have also reclaimed wisdom, moving it from the margins to somewhere near the center of scholarly interest.[8] This book itself is a reflection of this interest; introductions to biblical wisdom literature now constitute an important genre in biblical studies.

How should we assess biblical wisdom's place within the larger history of wisdom? Scholars have long recognized that ancient Israel was vigorously engaged with the intellectual discourse of its own "international" setting. The structure, form, and content of the canonical works—Proverbs, Job, and Ecclesiastes—is in various ways similar to wisdom texts from Egyptian and Mesopotamian wisdom traditions. Sirach and Wisdom of Solomon may be described as "Greek wisdom books,"[9] not only because extant copies are written in Greek, but also because they are deeply enmeshed in Hellenistic philosophy. Whether we think of Israelite sages as appropriating, adapting, and/or transforming the ideas they encountered in their world, there can be no doubt that they considered the pursuit of wisdom a cross-cultural enterprise. The questions life pressed on them—about life and death, good and evil, justice and injustice, wealth and poverty—were so challenging that they could not afford to think and live in silos. If they were to know "how the world is made and holds together" (Wis 7:17), they had to be thinkers who participated in the wider intellectual economy.

Modern biblical scholars have reflected on ancient Israel's cross-cultural and transhistorical approach to wisdom, but we have yet to explore in any substantive way biblical wisdom's place in the wider history of wisdom. The arc of this history is long and steadily lengthening. Alongside biblical wisdom, we should compare and contrast not only pre-Socratic and post-Socratic philosophers, but also Buddhist wisdom, such as the Heart and Diamond Sutras that are roughly historically contiguous.[10] Beyond ancient Western and Eastern philosophies, we should explore what biblical wisdom might draw from and contribute to African philosophical thought, much of which is rooted in a history of diasporic experience not unlike that of ancient Israel.[11] The history of wisdom expands with the history of history: from Augustine to Aquinas, from the Renaissance to Romanticism, from Descartes to Kant, from post modernism to post humanism. Once lodged primarily in religious and philosophical studies, the search for the source and substance of wisdom has become transdisciplinary in ways ancient sages could not have imagined. Psychology, cognitive science, and neurotheology each in its way has probed the science of wisdom. It is interesting, and humbling, to discover that scholars outside our specialized (read, *siloed*) field of biblical study are reading us more than we are reading them.[12]

Introductions to biblical wisdom literature have not covered this wider history of wisdom. The introduction you are reading now is no exception. There are obvious practical reasons why we have limited our focus to these five substantive, wisdom texts in the Hebrew Bible and Apocrypha, not least the length and heft (and cost) of the book that would be necessary to cover the material. But our work is the poorer for the omission. Ancient Israel's sages recognized the need to be in conversation with wider fields of knowledge in their world. Indeed, the sage who gave us the Wisdom of Solomon reports that the king had a vast knowledge of astronomy, zoology, physics, biology, psychology, and medicine (Wis 7:17-20). If the history of wisdom can be seen as "a never-ending battle between the forces of theology [Wisdom with a capital *W*] and those of secularization [wisdom with a small *w*]," as Hall suggests, then should we not place the insights of biblical wisdom into Socratic-like dialogue with all seekers of wisdom, just as the authors of Proverbs, Job, Ecclesiastes, Sirach, and Wisdom have done in their respective worlds?[13]

I take some comfort in the fact that introductions are necessarily first steps, not final stops. They are meant to begin a process of thinking that is open to new discoveries, not to close thinking down or hem it in with unexamined certainties. For such a journey, I suggest the Joban question nested in the center of these five old texts remains a critical beginning point for the modern world: Where can wisdom be found? (Job 28:12).

For Further Reading:

Introductions to Old Testament Wisdom

Brown, W. B. *Character in Crisis: A Fresh Approach to the Wisdom Literature of the Old Testament.* Grand Rapids, MI: William B. Eerdmans, 1996.

———. *Wisdom's Wonder: Character, Creation, and Crisis in the Bible's Wisdom Literature.* Grand Rapids, MI: William B. Eerdmans, 2014.

Clifford, R. J. *The Wisdom Literature.* Interpreting Biblical Texts. Nashville: Abingdon, 1998.

Collins, J. J. *Jewish Wisdom in the Hellenistic Age*. The Old Testament Library. Louisville, KY: Westminster John Knox, 1997.

Crenshaw, J. L. *Old Testament Wisdom: An Introduction*. Rev. ed. Louisville, KY: Westminster John Knox, 2010.

Dell, K. *Get Wisdom, Get Insight: An Introduction to Israel's Wisdom Literature*. Macon, GA: Smyth & Helwys, 2000.

Gammie, J. G., and L. G. Perdue, eds. *The Sage in Israel and the Ancient Near East*. Winona Lake, IN: Eisenbrauns, 1990.

Jarick, J., ed. *Perspectives on Israelite Wisdom: Proceedings of the Oxford Old Testament Seminar*. London: Bloomsbury T & T Clark, 2016.

Kampen, J. *Wisdom Literature*. Eerdman's Commentaries on the Dead Sea Scrolls. Grand Rapids, MI: William B. Eerdmans, 2011.

Murphy, R. *The Tree of Life: An Exploration of Biblical Wisdom Literature*. 3rd ed. Grand Rapids, MI: William B. Eerdmans, 2002.

Penchansky, D. *Understanding Wisdom Literature: Conflict and Dissonance in the Hebrew Text*. Grand Rapids, MI: William B. Eerdmans, 2012.

Perdue, L. G. *The Sword and the Stylus: An Introduction to Wisdom in the Age of Empires*. Grand Rapids, MI: William B. Eerdmans, 2008.

———.*Wisdom Literature: A Theological History*. Louisville, KY: Westminster John Knox, 2007.

Rad, Gerhard von. *Wisdom in Israel*. Nashville: Abingdon, 1972.

Sneed, M. *The Social World of the Sages: An Introduction to Israelite and Jewish Wisdom Literature*. Minneapolis: Fortress, 2015.

Weeks, S. *An Introduction to the Study of Wisdom Literature*. London: T & T Clark, 2010.

Westermann, C. *Roots of Wisdom: The Oldest Proverbs of Israel and Other Peoples*. Louisville, KY: Westminster Kohn Knox, 1999.

Chapter 1

Proverbs

"Wisdom Begins with the Fear of the Lord"

A proverb, one might say, is a ruin which stands on the site of an old story and in which a moral twines about a happening like ivy around a wall.

Walter Benjamin[1]

Behind every proverb there is a story, or to be more accurate, a long history of stories populated by life experiences and aggregate knowledge. The origin of these stories will likely have been long since forgotten, but kernels of truth fossilize into wisdom passed from one generation to the next. Twined around these kernels, as Walter Benjamin suggests in the citation above, is a moral lesson concerning what is right and wrong, what to do and what not to do, if one wishes to live well. The book of Proverbs is the "ivy around the wall" of ancient Israel's moral construct for what is "righteous, just, and full of integrity" (Prov 1:3).

The final form of the book, with all but one of the major text units introduced by a title or superscription, provides an instructive entry into four major interpretive issues: (1) composition history; (2) literary forms; (3) sociopolitical context; and (4) thematic coherence.

9

Proverbs

1:1–9:18	"The proverbs of Solomon King David's son, from Israel" (1:1)
10:1–22:16	"The proverbs of Solomon" (10:1)
22:17–24:22	"The words of the wise" (22:17)
24:23-34	"These are also the sayings of the wise" (24:23)
25:1–29:27	"These are also proverbs of Solomon, copied by the men of Hezekiah, king of Judah" (25:1)
30:1-33	"The words of Agur, Jakeh's son" (30:1)
31:1-9	"The words of King Lemuel of Massa, which his mother taught him" (31:1)
31:10-31	An untitled poem, structured as an acrostic (alphabetic) hymn, praising the "competent wife"

Composition History

The different introductions indicate that this book is a compilation of texts that have been stitched together over time. That parts are attributed to Solomon (1:1; 10:1; 25:1) is more a recognition of his legendary embodiment of "the spirit of wisdom" exemplified by Moses and Joshua than a claim that he authored these texts (Deut 34:9; cf. 1 Kgs 2:6; 3:3-28; 4:29-34; 10:1-25). The long legacy of Solomon's wisdom is evident both within this book, in its inclusion of the "copy work" attributed to Hezekiah's officials (Prov 25:1), who would have been active some two centuries after Solomon's death, and in biblical (Eccl 1:1) and deuterocanonical books that extend the memory of Solomon's wisdom into the first century CE (Sir 47:12-17; Wis 7–9) and well beyond.[2] A part of this legacy connects Solomon's wisdom with that of other sages in the Eastern Mediterranean world (1Kgs 5:1-18), which suggests that a collection called "the proverbs of Solomon" will likely draw upon an international wisdom discourse. The book of Proverbs confirms this. The section introduced as the "sayings of the wise" (22:17–24:22) shows a creative dependence on the second millennium Egyptian text, "The Instruction of Amenemope."[3] Both "the words of Agur, Jakeh's son" (30:1-33) and "the words of King Lemuel" (31:1-9) are attributed to a foreigner from Massa (*māssa'*), a region in Arabia.[4] We may deduce from this variegated collection that in ancient Israel, as in every place where *Homo sapiens* ("wise persons") lived, the pursuit of wisdom was instinctive.

To read Proverbs front to back, following the sequence of chapters preserved in its final form, is to recognize that this book has a complex compositional history spanning centuries. Because there are no confirmable historical markers, scholars typically locate the Solomonic collections (10:1–22:16; 25:1–29:27) in the latter part of the First Temple period (eighth to seventh century BCE). This earliest form was then enlarged by the addition of other collections, with the framing pieces (chapters 1–9 and 31) likely added in the early Persian period (538–333 BCE). The Septuagint (LXX) sequences parts of the collection differently (22:17–24:22 → 30:1-14 → 24:23-34 → 30:15-33 → 31:1-9 → 25:1–29:27 → 31:10-31), an indication that the final form of the book remained in flux during the Hellenistic period (323–331 BCE).

This collection of "proverbs" and "words" and "sayings," wisdom added to wisdom over the span of at least four centuries, represents ancient Israel's participation in an international intellectual economy. In the Western world, we tend to think *philosophia* ("love of wisdom") begins with Plato and Aristotle in ancient Greece. As the entry point into the Old Testament's wisdom literature, Proverbs is a reminder that the quest to understand the nature of the world and the purpose of life transcends all geographical and cultural boundaries.[5] Proverbs 18:15a puts it this way: "The mind of an intelligent person goes about acquiring knowledge" (author's translation).

Literary Forms

The most distinctive literary form in wisdom literature is the "proverb" (*māšāl*). The word appears in the title of the first two collections (1:1;

10:1), which illustrate the various forms proverbs take. The first collection consists of ten speeches (1:8-19; 2:1-22; 3:1-12; 3:21-35; 4:1-9; 4:10-19; 4:20-27; 5:1-23; 6:20-35; 7:1-27), couched as instructions, admonitions, warnings, and rebukes from a teacher, variously characterized, whose personal authority should persuade the hearer to heed the counsel offered. Proverbs 1:8-19 exemplifies parental advice to a child: "My son, don't let sinners entice you, . . . don't go on the path with them . . . because their feet run to evil" (vv. 10, 15, 16). If children accept this counsel, they will follow the "good course" of "righteousness and justice, as well as integrity" (2:9); they will "find wisdom" and "gain understanding" (3:13); and their reward will be a long life of "well-being" (3:2), a "glorious crown" (4:9) that symbolizes the nobility of a virtuous life. Alternatively, the child may be tempted to heed the siren call of seduction, personified as the "mysterious woman" whose "slick words" (2:16) "drip honey" (5:3) but ensnare the one who partakes in disgrace that cannot be erased (6:33). Embedded within these ten speeches are the words of another teacher, personified now as Woman Wisdom, who counters the "mysterious woman," first by mocking those who refuse wisdom's invitation (1:20-33), then by delighting in those who are wise enough to "keep to my ways" (8:32), enter into her house, and feast on the food and wine at her bounteous table (9:5).

The 375 proverbial sayings in the second collection (10:1–22:16) exemplify a more succinct literary form, typically one-line maxims, divided into parallel halves, that advocate inviolable truths by means of three primary rhetorical strategies. The dominant form of the sayings in Proverbs 10–15 utilizes an *antithetical parallelism* to draw a sharp contrast between two different ways of living. See the following contrasts, for example:

wise or foolish	"A wise child makes a father glad, but a foolish child brings sorrow to his mother." (10:1)
	"The skillful mind accepts commands, but a foolish talker is ruined." (10:8)
righteous or wicked	"The treasure of the wicked won't profit them, but righteousness rescues people from death." (10:2)

"The Lord doesn't let the righteous starve,
but he rejects the desires of wicked." (10:3)

lazy or diligent

"A hard worker is in charge,
while a lazy one will be sentenced to hard labor."
(12:24)

"The lazy have strong desires but receive nothing;
the appetite of the diligent is satisfied." (13:4)

kind or cruel

"Kind persons benefit themselves,
but cruel people harm themselves." (11:17)

"Those who despise their neighbors are sinners,
but happy are those who are kind to the needy."
(14:21)

honest or deceitful

"Those who state the truth speak justly,
but a false witness deceives." (12:17)

"A truthful witness saves lives,
but a deceiver proclaims lies." (14:25)

patience or impatience

"Patience leads to abundant understanding
but impatience leads to stupid mistakes." (14:29)

"Hotheads stir up conflict, but patient people
calm down strife." (15:18)

restrained or unrestrained
with words

"With lots of words comes wrongdoing, but
the wise restrain their lips." (10:19)

"People who watch their mouths guard their
lives, but those who open their lips are ruined."
(13:3)

greedy or gracious

"Those who give generously receive more,
but those who are stingy with what is
appropriate will grow needy." (11:24)

"Those who acquire things unjustly gain trouble
for their house, but those who hate bribes will
live." (15:27)

The sayings in Proverbs 16–22 are more often conveyed by a *synonymous parallelism* in which a truth is stated in the first half of the line then essentially repeated with similar words in the second half, for example:

A false witness won't go unpunished, and a liar won't escape. (19:5)

Laziness brings on deep sleep; a slacker goes hungry. (19:15)

The Lord detests false weights; deceptive scales aren't right. (20:23)

A variation of this form, often labeled progressive or synthetic parallelism, states a truth in the first half of the line then extends or intensifies its meaning in the second half, for example:

Gray hair is a crown of glory; it is found on the path of righteousness. (16:31)

Fools find no pleasure in understanding, but only in expressing their opinion. (18:2)

Those who are gracious to the poor lend to the Lord, and the Lord will fully repay them. (19:17)

Wine is a mocker; beer a carouser. Those it leads astray won't become wise. (20:1)

Integral to each of these types of one-line sayings is the assumption that an unambiguous truth is plain to see. It does not need to be argued, and compliance need not be commanded. Simple assertion, buttressed by the wisdom of collective experience, conveys its own imperative.

Scattered within and beyond these two collections are additional literary forms. "Better than" sayings teach that one thing is preferable to another. For example: "Better to be held in low regard and have a servant, than to be conceited and lack food" (12:9; cf. 15:16, 17; 16:8, 19; 19:1; 21:9; 25:7, 24; 27:5, 10c). Conditional sentences use an "if-then" construction to accent the connection between deed and consequence, for example: "If you find honey, eat just the right amount; otherwise, you'll get full and vomit it up" (25:16; cf. 23:13-15; 24:10-12, 14; 29:9, 12, 14). Rhetorical questions invite agreement with assumed answers, for example: "Do you see people who consider themselves wise? There is more hope for a fool than for them" (26:12; cf. 24:12; 29:20).

Numerical sayings catalogue social and natural phenomena, thus widening the perspective for understanding:

> There are six things that the Lord hates,
>> seven things detestable to him:
>> snobbish eyes,
>> a lying tongue,
>> hands that spill innocent blood,
>> a heart set on wicked plans,
>> feet that run quickly to evil,
>> a false witness who breathes lies,
>> and one who causes conflicts among relatives. (6:16-19; cf. 30:15-16,
>>> 18-19, 21, 23, 24-28, 29-31)

Metaphors and *similes* offer poetic analogies that engage and revitalize the imagination. For example: "Words spoken at the right time are like gold apples in a silver setting" (25:11; cf. 10:11, 20, 26; 11:22; 12:4, 18; 16:24; 17:8, 22; 18:4, 8; 22:14; 23:27-28; 25:12, 18; 26:11, 18-19; 28:3, 15).

A previous generation of scholarship made much of the difference between the longer speeches that dominate in Proverbs 1–9, which are framed by a distinctive theological linkage between "the beginning of wisdom" and the "fear of the Lord" (1:7; 9:10), and the shorter sentence forms that dominate in the other collections of the book, which were thought to be grounded primarily in empirical and practical observations. The sentence forms were widely regarded as exemplars of older wisdom, which was rooted in Near Eastern antecedent traditions. The speeches, however, were thought to be ancient Israel's later theologized adaptation of international wisdom discourse. This distinction has largely collapsed for two reasons.

First, it is now clear that ancient Near Eastern texts routinely connected wisdom with the gods who created the world and endowed it with principles of order and justice. Sumerian texts from the third millennium BCE report that Enki/Ea, the god of wisdom who organizes the earth, sent Adapa, the first of seven antediluvian "super sages" (*apkallu*), to teach the arts of civilization (*me*) to human beings. In the postdiluvian age,

Ziusudra (known in Mesopotamian texts as Atrahasis, "extra wise," and Utnapishtam) resumes Adapa's role as the divine sage who has access to the wisdom that keeps the world operating in accord with the design put in place by the gods.[6] In Egyptian wisdom texts and iconography, the goddess of truth and justice (*ma`at*) sets the moral order of the cosmos to which humans must conform, if they are to live successfully. In short, there was no "secular" understanding of life in the ancient world. Every aspect of one's existence from birth to death to afterlife was inextricably tied to divine decision. The notion that "the beginning of wisdom is the fear of the LORD" (9:10) may be a distinctively Israelite conception (see below), but it draws upon a religious worldview that has deep roots in contiguous cultures.[7]

Second, neither in ancient Near Eastern wisdom texts nor in Proverbs is there a strong distinction between "practical" wisdom and "religious" wisdom. According to Sumerian texts, the one hundred-plus me's created and transmitted by the gods to human beings for the purpose of keeping order in the world included a wide assortment of practical skills in areas such as music, metalworking, weaving, and building.[8] Adapa, for example, is said to demonstrate the technique of baking and fishing to the people of Eridu.[9] Alongside these practical skills, however, the gods also dispensed wisdom concerning the cultic prescriptions for proper worship.[10] Learning how to worship, no less than learning how to bake, fish, and build, was one of the arts essential for a prosperous life.

In Proverbs, the "fear of the LORD" is not only the beginning of wisdom in an abstract theological sense, as one might suppose from a thin reading of Proverbs 1–9; it is also the source of very pragmatic and practical benefits, such as longevity (10:27), "confidence" (14:26), and material prosperity (15:16; 22:4). Moreover, "YHWH sayings" are not limited to Proverbs 1–9 but occur throughout the book (e.g., 16:1, 2, 9; 17:3; 20:24, 27; 21:31; 28:5, 25; 29:25, 26), a repeating reminder that wise and moral behavior—"righteousness and justice, as well as integrity" (2:9; cf. 1:9)—is necessarily generated, informed, corrected, and sustained by devotion to the God who tuned the world to these requisite virtues.

Sociopolitical Context

The discreet collections and the various literary forms are indicative of the different social and political contexts in which proverbial material functioned in ancient Israel. Two primary contexts may be singled out: 1. the family setting; and 2. the royal court setting.

(1) The speeches in Proverbs 1–9 reflect a *family setting* in which a parent endeavors to shape a child's intellectual and moral development. This domestic setting for wisdom reflects the dynamics of Israel's pre-state period, when parents were the locus of authority for a child's education and character formation. Persistent appeals, such as, "My son, pay attention to my wisdom. Bend your ear to what I know" (5:1; cf. 1:6, 10, 15; 2:1; 3:1, 11, 21; 4:1, 11, 20; 5:7; 6:1, 3, 20), impart long-standing communal values. The template for these values is 1:2-7, which serves as an introduction to both the first collection and to the book as a whole:

> For learning about wisdom [*ḥokmâ*] and instruction [*mûsār*],
>> for understanding words of insight [*bînâ*],
>
> for gaining instruction [*mûsar*] in wise dealing,
>> righteousness [*ṣedek*], justice [*mišpāṭ*], and equity [*mêšārîm*];
>
> to teach shrewdness [*'ormâ*] to the simple,
>> knowledge [*da'at*] and prudence [*mězimmâ*]to the young—
>
> let the wise also hear and gain in learning [*leqaḥ*],
>> and the discerning acquire skill [*taḥbulôt*],
>
> to understand a proverb and a figure,
>> the words of the wise and their riddles.
>
> The fear of the Lord is the beginning of knowledge [*dā'at*];
>> fools despise wisdom [*ḥokmâ*] and instruction [*mûsār*]. (1:2-7 NRSV)

To become productive and responsible members of society, all persons—the "simple" the "young," and even the "wise" (1:4-5)—must acquire and develop the following:

- "Wisdom" (*ḥokmâ*, v. 2), "knowledge" (*da'at*, vv. 4, 7), and "understanding" (*bînâ*, v. 2). In the broadest sense, "knowledge" is information, facts, data, in sum, virtually anything a person acquires through thinking or experience. "Understanding" is discernment, the result of a cognitive process of analyzing and interpreting information in a way that clarifies meaning that may lie beneath the surface. "Wisdom" is a combination of knowledge elevated to expertise and understanding enacted in moral and ethical behavior. To acquire wisdom is to be able to weigh all options, to decide which is morally compelling, and to act accordingly.[11]

- "Instruction" (*mûsār*, vv. 2, 3, 7) and "learning" (*leqaḥ*, v. 5). *Mûsār* is the "instruction," "discipline," or "correction" the teacher gives to the student. It is authoritative because it comes from a superior to an inferior; and compliance is obligatory because the learner (the child) is morally bound to submit to the teacher (the parent). "Learning" has to do more with how wisdom is to be communicated to others than with how it is acquired. The word usually connotes erudition or eloquence. Those who obtain wisdom aspire to communicate truth persuasively.

- "Righteousness" (*ṣedek*, v. 3), "justice" (*mišpāṭ*, v. 3), and "equity" (*mêšārîm*, v. 3). All three terms have to do with ethical behavior, although they have slightly different nuances. "Righteous" is the quality ascribed to one whose life in community with others complies with a normative code of ethics. The term closely aligns with "equity," which conveys the sense of being "straight" or "upright," and by extension, being "honest" and "truthful." "Justice" is a broad term that applies to every aspect of the moral vision that requires ethical behavior in all areas of life, individual and communal, economic and political. Where justice is present it must be secured and sustained. Where it is lacking, it must be restored and reinforced.

- "Shrewdness" (*'ormâ*, v. 4) and "prudence" (*mĕzimmâ*, v. 4). "Shrewdness" (*'ormâ*) refers to cunning or guile, which for the wise means having the maturity to see clearly ultimate objectives and to craft the right strategy to accomplish them. The Hebrew root from which "prudence" derives (*zāmam*) means "plan" or "devise." In the context of teaching the young, it is the exhortation to beginners to think for themselves, to be confident about their capacity to seek and obtain wisdom wherever it may be found (cf. Prov 8:12).

- "Skill" (*taḥbulôt*, v. 5). To acquire "skills" in the context of wisdom thought means to have the capacity to steer a successful course through whatever obstacles may lie ahead. The LXX translates the line as, "the discerning will acquire direction [*kybernēsin*]," and understands the term to be associated with the Hebrew words "rope" (of a ship; *ḥebel*), "sailor" (*ḥobēl*), and "mast" or "rigging" (*ḥibbēl*). The nautical imagery suggests "navigational skills," or in common parlance, "learning the ropes."[12]

Wisdom comprising the virtues above and learned in a familial context should be enacted in all areas of life, including, for example, being a good neighbor (3:27-31), marital fidelity (5:15-20), money lending (6:1-3), and diligent labor (6:6-11). The taproot of the learning and insight required to navigate each of these areas successfully is the wisdom that comes from devotion to God (1:7; 2:6; 9:10). Thus the parent's instruction, like that of Woman Wisdom, the parental character who personifies the very wisdom of God (1:20-33; 8:1-36; 9:1-17), makes a common appeal: "Don't reject the instruction of the LORD, my son; don't despise his correction. The LORD loves those he corrects, just like a father" (3:11-12).

(2) The Solomonic collection (10:1–22:16), "the words" (22:17–24:22) and "sayings" (24:23-34) of the wise, and the other proverbs "copied by the men of Hezekiah, king of Judah" (25:1–29:27), reflect a royal or court *setting* for instruction in wisdom.[13] Envisioned is the historical period of the monarchy, when the center of power and authority in Israel shifted from the family to the state, the official responsibility for education from the parent to a professional class of scribes and sages. The content of these various collections suggests that by the time of Hezekiah's reign, if not earlier, the national and international affairs of state required that those who served the king be educated in a wide range of matters, including:

table etiquette:

> When you sit down to dine with a ruler,
>> carefully consider what is in front of you.
>
> Place a knife at your throat
>> to control your appetite.
>
> Don't long for the ruler's delicacies;
>> the food misleads.
>
> Don't wear yourself out trying to get rich;
>> be smart enough to stop.
>
> When your eyes fly to wealth
>> it is gone; it grows wings
>> like an eagle and flies heavenward.
>
> Don't eat food with stingy people;
>> don't long for their delicacies,
>> because they are like a hair in the throat.
>
> They say to you, "Eat and drink!"
>> but they don't mean it.
>
> You will eat scraps and vomit them out.
>> You will waste your pleasant words. (23:1-8)

the administration of impartial justice for the accused:

> Those who acquire things unjustly gain trouble for their house,
>> but those who hate bribes will live. (15:27)
>
> Favoring the wicked is not good:
>> it denies justice to the righteous. (18:5; cf. 15:27; 17:15, 23; 18:17;
>> 24:23b; 28:21)

economic policy, especially the obligation to the poor and disenfranchised:

> Those who exploit the powerless anger their maker,
>> while those who are kind to the poor honor God. (14:31)

> Those who mock the poor insult their maker,
>> those who rejoice in disaster won't go unpunished. (17:5)

> Don't steal from the poor, because they are poor.
> Don't oppress the needy in the gate.
> The Lord will take up their case
>> and press the life out of those who oppress them. (22:22-23; cf. 1:23;
>>> 15:25; 19:17)

the cult:

> The Lord detests the sacrifices of the wicked,
>> but favors the prayers of those who do right. (15:8)

> Those who turn their ears from hearing Instruction—
>> even their prayers will be detested. (28:9; cf. 15:29; 17:1 21:3, 27)

The king himself should wear wisdom like a crown (25:2), thus modeling the wisdom required in his court (16:10-15). He is expected to invite instruction and to be receptive to critique (28:3, 15-16; 29:4, 12, 14). According to the Lemuel collection (31:1-9), the king is subject to the admonitions of his mother, who warns him that excessive consumption of alcohol will compromise his ability to speak clearly on behalf of the poor and needy who appeal for justice.

By and large, court wisdom promotes a politically and theologically conservative perspective on the world, reflecting the institutional status of the sages. Through antithetical proverbs they envision a world where choices are clear and their consequences unambiguous. One is *either* righteous *or* wicked, wise *or* foolish, and the rewards for choosing either path of life are predictably etched into the cosmic order by God, whom the king faithfully serves.[14] There is little room and virtually no encouragement in court wisdom for questions or dissent. Edifying speech is prized (e.g., 10:11, 21; 15:4; 16:21, 23, 24), for "the lips of the wise know what is acceptable" (10:32), but best of all, especially in the face of moral complexities, is silence (10:19; 11:12b; 12:23; 13:3; 17:28), rooted in the abiding truth that the one who trusts God's inscrutable wisdom is safe (14:26; 16:3, 20; 18:10; 29:25), whatever the limits of human understanding (16:1, 9; 19:21; 21:30-31). There is sparing acknowledgment that the system of rewards and punishments sometimes seems upside down (30:21-23) and that what is incomprehensible may drive one more to lament than praise (30:1-4), but such thoughts are placed on the lips of foreigners, perhaps a subtle suggestion that their wisdom has merit but is not the norm. On this point, however, the sages who speak in Proverbs are not the only voices sitting at wisdom's table. Job (represented as another foreigner, Job 1:1) will advance the lament and the protest that is barely audible in Proverbs; Qohelet will press this lament to its outermost boundaries, where skepticism demands a hearing.

Thematic Coherence

Because of its anthological character, scholars generally concede that Proverbs lacks any overarching thematic coherence. Superscriptions identify the beginning and ending of different sections, as noted previously; thematic emphases frame certain sections (e.g., "the fear of the Lord" in chapters 1–9) and cluster together in others (e.g., righteousness and wickedness in 10:1–15:33; kingship in 16:10-15; 28:1–29:27). Repetitions, catchwords, and other rhetorical devices create sophisticated literary subunits within the collection (e.g., chapters 25–27). For all these structural and thematic markers, however, the book itself seems intentionally to thwart the search for a rationale that explains its final arrangement. As one scholar observes, Proverbs exhibits a "sweet disorder."[15]

The absence of a unifying structural design should not, however, be understood as a deficiency. To the contrary, Proverbs' sweet disorder introduces an important characteristic of Israelite thought that will become increasingly clear in our survey of the rest of this corpus of literature: the quest for wisdom was a process of thinking about thinking that resisted closure, for knowledge was itself always a moving target, a journey more than a destination. In its final form, Proverbs illustrates this in various ways.

22

(1) The intellectualization of piety (Prov 10–31) is combined with, not separated from, the piety of intellectualism (Prov 1–9). Wisdom in Proverbs develops in stages. The short maxims in Proverbs 10–29 constitute the first and earliest stage, when the pursuit of wisdom was primarily an intellectual exercise in thinking about pragmatic matters. It was not thinking divorced from trust in God's overarching providence and provision, but it did not assume that piety was a substitute for prudence. To be safe from danger, one should avoid conflict (14:16); to be prosperous, one should protect things of value (21:20) and secure their inheritance for posterity (17:2); to gain the respect and favor of others, one should be honest and forthright in all relationships (15:21, 24); to be persuasive in disagreements, one should develop verbal skills (10:13; 16:21). In sum, the wisdom in Proverbs 10–31 affirms the importance of human agency within the divine economy, the near-autonomous human capacity to think through the issues of life and resolve them satisfactorily without direct divine intervention, even if only in a limited way.[16]

The ten lessons in Proverbs 1–9 represent a second stage in the development of Israelite wisdom, which foregrounds piety rather than human intellect, dedication to God rather than acquisition of knowledge, and moral virtue rather than material prosperity. An excerpt from the third lecture provides an apt illustration:

> Trust in the Lord with all your heart;
> > don't rely on your own intelligence.
> Know him in all your paths,
> > and he will keep your ways straight.
> Don't consider yourself wise.
> > Fear the Lord and turn away from evil.
> Then your body will be healthy
> > and your bones strengthened.
> Honor the Lord with your wealth
> > and with the first of all your crops.
> Then your barns will be filled with plenty,
> > and your vats will burst with wine. (3:5-10)

To be safe from danger one should certainly avoid conflict, but more important is the security that comes from trusting God (3:5); to attain knowledge by human reasoning enables good choices when navigating the obstacles in life, but the better part of wisdom is the humility to recognize that it is God who clears the way forward (3:6); to have confidence in one's ability to effect change is admirable, but reverence for God mitigates self-glorification (3:7-8); to secure wealth for future generations is always smart, but the wise will recognize abundance as a summons to honor God (3:9-10). Devotion to God does not deny the role of human agency in the intellectual economy of life, but it does render it subordinate to a higher power.

The sages who added Proverbs 1–9 to the Solomonic collection provided the first commentary on the intellectualization of piety in ancient Israel. From their perspective, a proper understanding of wisdom required the "fear of the Lord." We will examine this perspective below, but at this juncture it is important to note that these sages were modeling the very intellectual process they were critiquing. They were thinking about thinking. Even as they advocated piety as a precondition for obtaining wisdom, they were engaging in an intellectual exercise that subjected observations about the way the world works to rigorous review and analysis.[17] Although it may not have been their primary objective, their contribution to the final form of Proverbs demonstrates that in ancient Israel wisdom was more about discussion and debate than settled conclusions.

(2) "The fear of the Lord is the beginning of knowledge" (Prov 1:7 NRSV; cf. Prov 9:10; 15:33; Job 28:28; Ps 111:10; Sir 1:14, 16, 18, 20, 27; 19:20; 21:11). The sages who provided the prologue in 1:2-7 understood it to be the key for interpreting not only chapters 1–9 but also the entire book. The concluding verse of this prologue could be interpreted as the elusive thematic thread that ties the discreet sections into a unified whole: "Wisdom begins with the fear of the Lord." The three iterations of this maxim in Proverbs (1:7; 9:10; 15:33)[18] affirm essentially the same truth: the starting point for obtaining wisdom is an awareness of God's presence that evokes what Aristotle and Plato called the pathos of "wonder" (*to thaumazein*).[19] Wonder is the catalyst for curiosity. Israel's psalmists express a similar pathos with poetic imagination:

Lord, our Lord, how majestic

    is your name throughout the earth! . . .

When I look up at your skies,

    at what your fingers have made—

    the moon and the stars

    that you set firmly in place—

        what are human beings that you think about them;

        what are human beings that you pay attention to them?

        (Ps 8:1, 3-4)

Is a sense of God's presence available to everyone in equal measure, as the sages suggest in the prologue (1:4-5), then repeatedly throughout the ten lectures (e.g., 1:20-22; 8:1-5; 9:4), or are some excluded either by choice or design (e.g., 1:24-31; 8:35-36; 9:13-18)? Proverbs 1–9 entertains the questions but quenches curiosity by affirming a tautology: "the fear of the LORD is the beginning of knowledge" (1:7 NRSV); "the beginning of wisdom is the fear of the LORD" (9:10). What Proverbs 1–9 regards as axiomatic—wisdom is available to all who seek wisdom, and all who seek wisdom will find wisdom—the Solomonic collection presents as a truth bifurcated by reality: the wise are not foolish, and the foolish are not wise; the righteous are not wicked, and the wicked are not righteous; the good is not evil, and the evil is not good; the gracious are not greedy, and the greedy are not gracious (see the antithetical proverbs in chapters 10–15).

Given the debate engendered by these two stages in the growth of wisdom, perhaps it should not surprise that a later scribe appends a fatigued lament:

I'm tired, God;

    I'm tired, God, and I'm exhausted.

Actually, I'm too stupid to be human,

    a man without understanding.

I haven't learned wisdom,

    nor do I have knowledge of the holy one. (30:1-3)

And yet still another appendix (31:10-31) counters despair by reaffirming the motto of the book. The "woman of strength" (*'ēšēt ḥayîl*, v. 10, author's translation) embodies the virtues Proverbs promotes from beginning to end. She "reaches out to the needy" (v. 20), and "her mouth is full of wisdom" (*ḥokmâ*, v. 26). Such a woman, Proverbs concludes, and all who like her "fear the Lord," "is to be praised" (v. 30).

The final form of the book promotes the "fear of the Lord" as the beginning of wisdom. But the reader of Proverbs 1–31 knows that the journey from beginning to end is neither straightforward nor uncomplicated. There is a generating tension that will not be resolved between wisdom as piety and piety as wisdom, between those who can find the beginning of the path toward wisdom and those who cannot. The prologue has in fact already alerted readers to the challenge presented by "the words of the wise and their riddles" (*dibrê ḥăkāmîm wĕḥîdōt*; 1:6 NRSV). Riddles (CEB: "puzzles") are statements that are obscure, perhaps even irrational on the surface. They require and invite deciphering. As a still later sage will put the matter, those who would be wise must learn "to live with the puzzles" (*ainigmasi*, literally, "enigmas)" of life in relation to God (Sir 39:3).

(3) God never speaks in Proverbs, a characteristic that distinguishes this book and wisdom literature in general from the Pentateuch and the prophets.[20] In the Pentateuchal narrative, God is a major character who intervenes directly by speech and action in the unfolding drama. In prophetic literature, prophets typically introduce their speeches with the phrase, "Thus says the Lord," a messenger formula that signals they have come from God's presence and deliver God's words, not their own. When compared with these parts of the Old Testament, Proverbs can justifiably be called humanistic literature; its primary focus is not on divine revelation but on human acquisition of knowledge and its ethical imperatives for everyday life. Even so, at what was likely the latest editorial stage of the book, sages spliced into the ten lectures a series of interludes (1:20-33; 8:1-31; 9:1-18) that personify wisdom as a woman whose words summon people into the proximate presence of God. Woman Wisdom speaks wisdom that transcends human wisdom.[21] In doing so, she both identifies herself with God and distinguishes herself from God. Here again,

Proverbs is more about learning how to participate in dynamic reflections on wisdom than arriving at static conclusions.

Wisdom's speech in Proverbs 8 plays a central role in these reflections. In the first half of her speech (vv. 1-21), Wisdom describes herself as a teacher in search of students. She travels throughout cities and towns, palaces and temples (vv. 1-3), inviting all who will listen—the dull and the bright; the privileged and the disenfranchised—to heed her lessons about life, for what she has to offer is more valuable than gold (vv. 4-11). She identifies herself, "I [am] Wisdom" (*ḥokmâ*, v. 12a), and proclaims her own virtues, "prudence" (*'ormâ*), "knowledge" (*da'at*), and "discretion" (*mĕzimmâ*, v. 12), each of which the prologue introduces as essential for learning wisdom (see the discussion above on 1:2-7). Because she exemplifies the "fear of the Lord" (v. 12a), she possesses the counsel and competence that enables kings and rulers to govern with righteousness (*ṣedek*, vv. 14-16). She loves those who love her; their material prosperity is a reciprocal endowment of her riches and honor (vv. 17-21).

The most commented on part of Wisdom's speech (vv. 22-31) offers a striking correspondence between Wisdom's genesis and the creation of the cosmos as described in Genesis 1. This part of the speech is also the most complex and ambiguous:

> The Lord created me at the beginning of his way,
>> before his deeds long in the past.
>
> I was formed in ancient times,
>> at the beginning, before the earth was.
>
> When there were no watery depths, I was brought forth,
>> when there were no springs flowing with water.
>
> Before the mountains were settled,
>> before the hills, I was brought forth;
>> before God made the earth and the fields
>> or the first of the dry land.
>
> I was there when he established the heavens,
>> when he marked out the horizon on the deep sea,
>> when he thickened the clouds above,

> when he secured the fountains of the deep,
> when he set a limit for the sea,
>> so the water couldn't go beyond his command,
> when he marked out the earth's foundations.
> I was beside him as a master of crafts.
>> I was having fun,
>> smiling before him all the time,
>> frolicking with his inhabited earth
>> and delighting in the human race. (8:22-31)

On the one hand, Wisdom is primordial, preexistent, and preeminent, thus on some level coeval with God. Born before creation itself, Wisdom asserts that she was growing up "beside" God (v. 30), perhaps even a full participant with God in the creative act ("as a master of crafts," v. 30). On the other, Wisdom affirms that her genealogy begins with God. She is the first of God's creative acts; she comes from God and thus is subordinate to God. As if such contrasting statements do not make Wisdom's relationship to God ambiguous enough, verse 22 adds still another piece to the puzzle. The phrase, "The Lord created [*qānānî*] me," can also be translated, "The Lord *acquired* me,"[22] which would indicate that even for God wisdom was not an inherent or essential attribute. Like the learner who sits at the teacher's feet, God acquires wisdom through some sort of supernatural cognitive process. One commentator puts it this way:

> Though the author may not realize it, the underlying assumption is that prior to creation God was in stasis, his power only potential. He brought his power to actuality by acquiring wisdom. He acquired wisdom by creating it, drawing it from within, from the infinite potential for being that is inherent in Godhead.[23]

I do not cite these difficulties in order to resolve them, but instead to call attention to the generative complexity of the mosaic that is Proverbs.[24] Thinking about thinking was and remains an ongoing process of discernment about truths that are graspable but elusive.

In the midst of such ambiguity, however, it is important not to overlook another critical aspect of Woman Wisdom's speech. In verses 30-31, Wisdom speaks of her relationship to God in terms of mutual delight and laughter. "I was daily his delight" (NRSV)[25] Wisdom says, "[playing] [*mĕśaḥeqet*] before him all the time," indicating that God enjoys playing with wisdom like a parent delights in rolling around the floor with a laughing child (cf. Jer 31:20; Isa 66:12). As much as God has fun playing with Wisdom, Wisdom has fun playing with God and with humans (v. 31). Wisdom's speech ends with an accent on happiness. "Happy [*'aśrê*] are those who keep to my ways. . . . Happy [*'aśrê*] are those who listen to me" (8:32b, 34a; cf. 3:12-13).

For all its riddles and enigmas, its intrepid reflections on truth and knowledge, its resistance to settled conclusions, its incoherent coherence, Proverb invites its readers and learners to frolic in the pursuit of wisdom. To paraphrase Aristotle, even the gods enjoy thinking about thinking.[26]

For Further Reading

Akoto-Abutiate, D. *Proverbs and the African Tree of Life: Grafting Proverbs on to the Ghanaian Tree of Life.* Leiden: Brill, 2014.

Bland, D. *Proverbs and the Formation of Character.* Eugene, OR: Cascades, 2015.

Camp, C. *Wisdom and the Feminine in the Book of Proverbs.* Sheffield, UK: Almond Press, 1985.

Clifford, R. J. *Proverbs: A Commentary.* Old Testament Library. Louisville, KY: Westminster John Knox, 1999.

Dell, K. J. *The Book of Proverbs in Social and Theological Context.* Cambridge: Cambridge University Press, 2006.

Dell, K. J. and Will Kynes, eds. *Reading Proverbs Intertextually.* LHBOTS, London: Bloomsbury, forthcoming.

Fontaine, C. *Smooth Words: Women, Proverbs, and Performance in Biblical Wisdom.* Sheffield, UK: Almond Press, 2002.

Fox, M. *Proverbs 1–9.* Anchor Bible 18a. New Haven, CT: Yale University Press, 2000.

————. *Proverbs 10–31*. Anchor Bible 18b. New Haven, CT: Yale University Press, 2009.

Heim, K. M. *Poetic Imagination in Proverbs: Variant Repetitions and the Nature of Poetry*. Bulletin for Biblical Research Supplement 4. Winona Lake, IN: Eisenbrauns, 2013.

Lyu, S. M. *Righteousness in the Book of Proverbs*. Tübingen: Mohr Siebeck, 2012.

Moss, A. *Proverbs*. Readings: A New Biblical Commentary. Sheffield, UK: Sheffield Phoenix, 2015.

Sandoval, T. J. *The Discourse of Wealth and Poverty in the Book of Proverbs*. Leiden: Brill, 2006.

Schwáb, Z. *Toward an Interpretation of the Book of Proverbs: Selfishness and Secularity Reconsidered*. Journal of Theological Interpretation Supplement 7 (2013).

Stewart, A. W. *Poetic Ethics in Proverbs: Wisdom Literature and the Shaping of the Moral Self*. Cambridge: Cambridge University Press, 2015.

Washington, H. *Wealth and Poverty in the Instruction of Amenemope and the Hebrew Bible*. SBL Dissertation Series 142. Atlanta: Scholars Press, 1994.

Weeks, S. *Instruction and Imagery in Proverbs 1–9*. Oxford: Oxford University Press, 2007.

Yoder, C. *Wisdom as a Woman of Substance: A Socioeconomic Reading of Proverbs 1–9 and 31:10-31*. BZAW 304. Berlin: Walter de Gruyter, 2001.

Chapter 2

Job

"Wisdom, Where Can It Be Found?"

Proverbs begins and ends with a core affirmation: "Wisdom begins with the fear of the LORD" (Prov 1:7; 9:10; 31:30). On first reading, the book of Job endorses this affirmation. It begins with a prologue about a man named Job who steadfastly "reveres God and avoids evil" (1:1, 8; 2:3), despite horrendous and undeserved suffering, and ends with an epilogue recounting how God restored his fortunes and blessed him (42:7-17). A soliloquy near the center of the book stiches together its beginning and end into a harmonious affirmation of proverbial wisdom: "the fear of the LORD is wisdom; turning from evil is understanding" (28:28). The story is, however, far more complex than it first appears. The text cited in the title for this chapter—"Wisdom, where can it be found?"—is but a first clue that suffering like Job's had the capacity to turn the sages' affirmations into questions. Will Job's piety withstand the challenge of inexplicable suffering? Will the normative view of wisdom espoused in Proverbs—"the fear of the LORD turns away evil" (Prov 16:6)—withstand Job's challenge?

Form, Structure, and Genre

The frame of the book consists of a prose prologue (Job 1–2) and epilogue (42:7-17), which uses a combination of speech and action to tell the story of a righteous man who endures unbearable calamity and is rewarded by God for his unfailing fidelity. A narrator functions as the omniscient spectator (or scribe) who knows what truth the readers should discern. This truth is both simple—it is essentially beyond disagreement and dispute—and normative, that is, readers should agree to its authoritative claim on their lives. Job is "honest, a person of absolute integrity" (1:1), the narrator states categorically. He *is* "greater than all the people of the east" (1:3); when afflicted, he *does* fall on the ground, worship, and bless God (1:20-21); he *does not* sin (1:22); the Lord *does* "bless Job's latter days more than his former ones" (42:12); and Job *does* die "old and satisfied" (42:17).

The narrator privileges the principle of the story over the particulars. What is most important is the overarching truth that can be extracted and applied to any person in any time and place, not the individual circumstances that may raise questions about its specific application. Telltale signs that will soon complicate the story, especially the Adversary's questions about God's governance of the world (1:9) and God's admission that all that has turned Job's world upside down, including the deaths of his children, has happened "for no reason" (2:3), are temporarily muted (2:13). The narrator focuses instead on Job's unwavering piety: "Job did this [fear God] regularly" (1:5). An implicit universalizing also applies to the narrator's advocacy for a larger truth: this is who God always is; this is the way the world always works; this is the way everyone who fears God should always respond to misfortune.

This story is likely the oldest part of the book, originating in legendary tales from the ancient Near East of exemplary righteous persons who served Israel's sages as models for the wise behavior they wished their students to embrace (cf. Ezek 14:14, 20). It is not possible to date this version of the story with precision, but its depiction of Job's unquestioning affirmation of the sages' conventional retribution theology—God punishes the wicked and prospers the righteous—resonates with the optimism of the pre-exilic period, before the Babylonian conquest of Jerusalem.

The *center* of the book consists of an opening soliloquy by Job (Job 3), which sets in motion a series of dialogues between Job and his friends (Job 4–27), a second soliloquy by Job (29–31), and a final round of dialogues between Job and God (38:1–42:6). These chapters are written in poetry, not prose, and are dominated by the speech of the characters, not their actions. The speeches draw heavily on the genres of lament and disputation. Juxtaposed with the prologue/epilogue, they convey very different profiles of Job, the friends, and God. Instead of blessing without question the God who gives both the "good" and "bad" (1:21; 2:10), Job curses his life, and by implication the creator of all life (3:1-10), and repeatedly raises the question that demands an answer from every character in the ensuing dialogues, including God: "Why?" (3:11-26).

Upon first seeing the enormity of Job's suffering, the friends are silent and sympathetic (2:11-13). Once Job curses and questions God, they become increasingly strident. In three cycles of dialogues (4–14, 15–21, and 22–27), they move from counter-questions designed to comfort Job by assuring him that his righteousness will result in his ultimate vindication (4:2-6; 8:2-7; 11:2-6), to questions that warn and rebuke him for "doing away with the fear of God" (15:4 NRSV; cf. 18:4; 20:4-11), to questions that deny his innocence (22:1-11) and press him toward the only option left for those condemned as guilty: "Yield [*haskken*] to God, and be at peace" (22:21, author's translation; CEB: "Get along well with God").

One by one, Job refuses the wisdom of his friends. He insists that he is innocent (6:28-30, 9:21; 10:7; 16:7); the friends have whitewashed the truth with lies (13:4) and spoken deceitfully for the God they defend (13:7). He wonders if there is any place in heaven or on earth where the cries of the innocent can be justly addressed (16:18-22). He returns again and again to the idea that his only recourse is to summon God as a defendant to a courtroom trial where he could ask, "What are you doing?" (9:12), where an impartial "mediator" will assure that neither party has unfair advantage (9:33), where a "witness" in heaven will corroborate the truth of his testimony (16:19). Even if "there is no justice" in a court where the judge has already declared him guilty (19:6-7), Job clings to a faintly conceived hope that there is a "redeemer"—whether heavenly or human he does not know—who will come to his rescue (19:25-27). Toward that end, Job concludes his last extended speech by swearing his innocence and demanding that God respond to his subpoena to appear before the bar of justice: "Here's my signature; let the Almighty respond" (31:35).

The center of the book also profiles God differently. In the prologue and epilogue, God speaks *about* Job's exemplary fidelity but never *directly* addresses Job. After accepting the Adversary's wager by saying "There he is—within your power; only preserve his life" (2:6), God retreats in silence, never once uttering a word throughout the course of the dialogues between Job and his friends. When God speaks next, the words come "from the whirlwind" (38:1). The structure of God's first and only "dialogue" with Job (38:1–42:6) is clear—God has two speeches (38:1–39:40; 40:1-34 [Heb. 41:26]). Job offers two responses (40:3-5; 42:1-6), but the discourse is fraught with complexity. God speaks for 123 verses, Job for only nine. God comes *asking* his own questions, not *answering* the questions Job has persistently raised throughout the dialogues. In the first speech, the questions focus on God's "counsel" or "plan" (*'ēṣâ*) for the world (38:2), with specific attention to the cosmic boundaries (38:4-18), meteorological phenomena (38:19-38), and five pairs of animals (38:39–39:30). Job responds by saying "I'm of little worth," then places his hand over his mouth (40:3-5), a gesture that symbolizes his retreat into silence, although whether of shame, futility, or disapproval remains open to interpretation. In the second speech, the questions focus on God's governance of the world (*mišpāṭ*), with special attention to a sixth and final pair of animals, Behemoth (40:9-15) and Leviathan (41:1-34 [Heb. 40:25–41:26]). Job responds by stating what he now knows and sees about God and himself (42:1-6).

Numerous English translations render Job's final words in 42:6 as a confession of sin, for example, "Therefore I despise myself, and repent in dust and ashes" (NRSV). This reading is deeply ingrained in interpretive history, but grammatical ambiguities deny it the certainty it claims. Moreover, even with a conventional rendering of Job's response, there is no agreement between God and Job on a fundamental question that underlies the whole of their "conversation:" "Why have you [God] made me your target?" (7:20).

The wisdom conveyed in the poetic center of the book represents a different way of conceptualizing reality and its claims on readers than we find in the prose prologue. Beginning with chapter 3, the narrator disappears,

The story now advances through the speeches of one character to another, their entry onto the stage signaled by only a conventional recognition of the change of speaker: "Job said" (3:2); "Then Eliphaz, a native of Teman, responded" (4:1); "Job responded" (6:1); "Bildad from Shuah responded" (8:1); "Job responded" (9:1); "Zophar from Naamah responded" (11:1); "Job responded" (12:1); and so on. No third party steps into the middle of these conversations to critique them for the reader; dialogue, not monologue, sustains the story line. Instead of simple, authoritative assertions about the way the world works, the dialogues prize competing perspectives. Points of contradiction rather than agreement move the conversation from cycle to cycle, with roughly equal time allotted for each set of speakers to express themselves without interruption, until the conversation stalls at the end of chapter 27, with no party able to claim the upper hand. Job's three friends repeatedly assert the normative view of human suffering and God's justice. They urge Job toward truths they believe transcend all mitigating circumstances. While essentially agreeing with this norm, Job resolutely disagrees that it functions as it should for him, and he matches their assertions with his own questions and counter-assertions. He insists that if general assertions about God's justice cannot adequately address his particular pain—seven daughters and three sons dead "for no reason"— then all claims for a universalizing, transcendent justice are nothing more than a lie masquerading as truth. "Turn to me and be appalled," Job says to his friends, and "lay your hand over your mouth" (21:5; cf. 6:28; 13:17; 21:2). When he last speaks directly to his friends, his words indicate just how far apart they remain: "I will not agree that you are right. Until my dying day, I won't give up my integrity" (27:5).

It is possible the author of the dialogues is the same person who crafted the prologue/epilogue, in which case we should suppose that he chose to recast the traditional story about Job's unflinching fidelity to God by inserting these dialogues in the middle, thus strategically transforming a simple story into a much more complicated one. It is also possible that the dialogues should be attributed to a different and later author, who found the existent story of Job overly simplistic and woefully inadequate for the world in which he lived. A strong case can be made for locating this author in the time of the Babylonian exile (586–538 BCE), when the Israelites suffered massive destruction and losses that traumatized all explanation. By splicing the prologue and epilogue with the dispute between Job and his friends, this Joban poet explores the rift between the assurances of conventional wisdom and on-the-ground realities that threaten to nullify them.

Two later additions to the frame and center (Job 28, 32–37) betray the internal debate the book generated among the sages. The poem on wisdom in Job 28 is cast as an anonymous soliloquy. Unlike the previous speeches, it addresses no one directly, and it receives no response from the other characters in the book. It is generically similar to other sapiential poems that discuss wisdom's place in the world and the ability of humans to discover it (Prov 8; Sir 1, 24; Bar 3–4), but it differs from them by emphasizing wisdom's elusiveness rather than its availability. A twice-repeated question—"wisdom, where can it be found? (28:12, 20)—sets the table for the sage's answer: "humankind doesn't know" (28:13); "he [God] knows" (28:23). The last verse of the poem echoes the prologue's conventional commendation of Job's piety: "Look, the fear of the LORD is wisdom; turning from evil is understanding" (28:28; cf. 1:1, 8; 2:3). In the view of this later sage, perhaps writing from the Persian period when more traditional forms of wisdom thinking regained their dominance, the truly wise will accept without question what an inscrutable God gives and takes away (1:21), both the "good" and the "bad" (2:10). They will not follow the example of the Job of the dialogues, who complains and challenges God.

Whatever the sage's intention, the location of Job 28 does not resolve the existing tensions within the frame and center of the book; it adds to them. On the other side of this soliloquy, Job resumes his discourse, once again defending his integrity, protesting his mistreatment, and demanding that God respond to his quest for wisdom, however arrogant and inadequate it may be (29–31).

The speeches of Elihu (32–37), a fourth friend, elsewhere unmentioned, constitute a still later addition to the book, perhaps from a sage of the late Persian or early Hellenistic period. The substance of the speeches resonates with the intellectual climate of later wisdom texts like Ecclesiastes and Sirach and proto-apocalyptic texts like Daniel 1–6, which are set against a political backdrop of foreign domination that necessarily calls into question long-held convictions about God's power, justice, and compassion. Both Elihu's narrator (32:1-5) and Elihu as a character in his own right (32:6-22 and 33-37) suggest that what this story needs is a sage who can definitively "answer" ('*ānâ*) Job's questions (32:1, 3, 5, 6, 12, 17, 20). According to the narrator, Elihu's anger at the friends' failure compels him to speak (32:3, 5). When the constructed Elihu speaks for himself, however, he claims that he is motivated not by anger but by divine inspiration (32:8, 18; 33:4). *The* answer, Elihu argues, is that God has inscribed both divine silence (35:5-13) and human suffering into a revelatory process calibrated to invoke Job's confession (33:14-20) and awe (36:26–37:13; cf. Sir 36:26–37:13) before the Almighty.

Speaking for 159 verses, Elihu commands center stage for longer than any other character in the book, including God, except Job. His speeches, however, receive no response in the final form of the book. Couched as invitation to dialogue (33:5, 32), they effectively substitute monologue for dialogue and debate. Read against God's assessment of Job's friends in the epilogue—"you haven't spoken about me correctly" (42:7)—Elihu's "answer" invites further questions. Is his anger righteous and therefore worthy of imitation? Or, is it self-interested inspiration, folly masquerading as wisdom?

Job

A Man Named Job

The biblical story of Job is set in the land of Uz, presumably somewhere east of Israel, perhaps Edom (cf. Lam 4:21), but the reference is almost certainly to a location more fictional than real. The setting might just as well have been anywhere in the ancient world, for questions about suffering, divine justice, and the meaning of life generated an international wisdom discourse. Job-like characters play prominent roles in antecedent texts from ancient Egypt, Sumeria, Mesopotamia, Greece, and India.[1] These texts exhibit a cluster of conventional motifs that provide the background for reading the book of Job. In some cases, the biblical Job corresponds to these prototypes in expected ways; in others, the differences illuminate how ancient Israel's sages appropriated conventional wisdom for their own purposes. A select group of Mesopotamian texts may be singled out.

"A Man and His God," also known as the "Sumerian Job," describes the lamentations of a righteous sufferer, who has inexplicably lost his health, wealth, and respect. The burden of the sufferer's lament is a god who is indifferent to his troubles. Friends speak falsely about him and impugn his righteousness, the sufferer says, and the wicked plot evil against him, but his god does not intervene.

How long will you neglect me, leave me unprotected? . . .(l. 98)[2]

Unlike his biblical counterpart, the Sumerian Job accepts the counsel of the sages, who instruct him to give up his lament and conform to the truth of conventional wisdom: all suffering is the consequence of sin.

Never has a sinless child been born to its mother,
. . . a sinless workman has not existed from of old. . .(ll. 103-4)

The end of the text reports that when the sufferer confessed his sins, the god was pleased and rewarded him by turning his "suffering into joy" (l. 125).

"I Will Praise the Lord of Wisdom," also known as the "Babylonian Job," is the account of a noble person who has experienced a reversal of fortunes. He complains that his fidelity counts for nothing, because the gods have abandoned him.

I called to my god, but he did not show his face,
I prayed to my goddess, but she did not raise her head. (ll.4-5)[3]

Here again, lament gives way to compliance, as the sufferer concedes that Marduk's justice is simply inscrutable ("Who knows the will of the gods in heaven?" ll.36). The only thing this sufferer can know with certainty is that there will be no relief until he appeases Marduk with praise and thanksgiving (iv.42). There are "blasphemous implications"[4] in the poem that are similar to the biblical Job's, but the poem's predominant concern is the sufferer's eventual restoration. There is no attempt to explain the problem or to offer a solution, other than to affirm that the deity makes all things right in the end.

A third Mesopotamian text, "The Babylonian Theodicy," anticipates the impact of Job's personal suffering on the principles of justice that undergird world order. The text is cast as a dialogue between a sufferer and his companion, and the sufferer complains that he was abandoned as an orphan and left vulnerable to oppression and violence. The friend assures him that while suffering is common to all, those who remain steadfast will ultimately be better off for the experience (ll. 12-13, 18-19, 21-22).[5] The sufferer counters that his friend has not understood. The dialogue continues through repeated exchanges. The sufferer asserts the inexplicable reality of his plight. The friend responds with disputations and counterarguments. By the end of the poem, the two reach a resolution of sorts. The sufferer thanks his friend for his companionship and asks that he join him in petitioning the gods for mercy (ll. 287-88, 295-96).

There are parallels between "The Babylonian Theodicy" and Job, but there are also clear differences. Two differences deserve comment. First, the sufferer in "The Babylonian Theodicy" implies that the gods have failed him, but he never directly challenges them. He is satisfied to air his grievances before his friend and to wait in contrition for the merciful return of the gods who have inexplicably abandoned him. Job, by contrast, becomes increasingly determined to address his complaints and accusations directly to the God he holds responsible for his misfortune (e.g., 7:7-21; 10:1-17; 13:20-28; 30:20-31; 31:35-37). In the end, Job speaks of a change of heart (42:5-6), but it is far from clear that his words express contrition.[6] Second, the "dialogue" in "The Babylonian Theodicy" is between the sufferer and his companion. The gods never speak, never intervene, never have more than a spoken-about presence in the debate about pious suffering. By contrast, the Joban prologue and epilogue depict God as the first (1:7) and last (42:7) character to speak; the poetic center of the book contains two more lengthy divine speeches (38:1–40:2; 40:6–41:34 [Heb. 41:26]).

Of the Joban story's multiple departures from convention, none is more significant than the prominent speaking role Israel's sages give to God. The deities in other stories have only a figural or symbolic presence; they are depicted as either interested or disinterested spectators, not active participants. The biblical account not only makes God a full-fledged character in the story, but also it places on God's lips a concession about the moral senselessness of divine behavior—the ruination of a righteous person and his family "for no reason" (Job 2:3)—that is unprecedented in the sapiential tradition.

For No Reason

The poetic dialogues between Job and his friends represent the structural center of the book, but the brief exchange embedded in the prologue between God and the Adversary,[7] the first and only recorded conversation between these two parties in the Old Testament, is the fulcrum upon which the whole Joban story rests. Before God and the Adversary enter the story, Job, his wife, and his family live securely in an Edenic world. After God and the Adversary converse, the world they know vanishes, leaving in its wake the destruction of their possessions, the death of their children, and the trauma of psychic turmoil and physical affliction. Before God and the Adversary spoke with one another, there was no reason to question the integrity of either Job's piety or his prosperity. After they spoke, the story cannot find resolution until someone can satisfactorily answer the question posed by Job's last words in the prologue: "Should we accept only good from God and not accept evil?" (2:10 NJPS).[8] The rest of the book strains to explain how those who are "honest," of "absolute integrity," "revere God," and "avoid evil," can construct any sort of meaningful affirmation that connects the words *God*, *good*, and *evil*.

The dialogue unfolds in two stages (1:6-12; 2:1-6), each followed by the narrator's description of the mutually agreeable effects of these two conversations on Job and his family (1:13-22; 2:7-9). God initiates each exchange with a question, a subtle narrative device that signals God sets the agenda for the ensuing conversation. To the repeating question, "Where did you come from?" (1:7a; 2:2a), the Adversary twice responds that he has come into God's presence from "wandering throughout the earth" (1:7b; 2:2b). Twice God asks if the Adversary has "thought about my servant Job"; in each instance God indicates that Job is worthy of consideration because his righteousness exceeds that of anyone else the Adversary might inspect (1:8; 2:3).[9] God's affirmation of Job is essentially the same as the narrator's in 1:1-5 and does not substantially advance what we as readers already know. It is the Adversary's response to God that adds to the plotline.

In the first exchange, the Adversary raises two questions that shift the conversation from God's affirmation of Job to Job's motives for loyalty to God. First, a general, seemingly rhetorical question: "Does Job revere God for nothing [*ḥinnām*]?" (1:9). Without waiting for God's answer, the Adversary follows with a second question, now directed specifically to God, which he answers himself and challenges God to refute: "Haven't you fenced him in—his house and all he has—and blessed the work of his hands so that his possessions extend throughout the earth?" (1:10). He infers that God has so protected Job from adversity that it never occurs to him to do anything other than bless God. What if, the Adversary continues, you remove this protective border, stretch out your hand, and "strike" everything he has? When blessed by God, the Adversary does not doubt that Job will bless God in return. But when cursed by God, will Job not curse God in return? God responds by handing over Job and all that he has into the Adversary's hands, with the proviso that he must stop short of striking Job himself (1:11). In rapid succession four messengers announce a series of calamities that erase from Job's world his oxen, donkeys, sheep, camels, servants, and finally, his sons and daughters. Both the Adversary and God are portrayed as on-lookers; both watch to see how Job will respond to his losses. When the narrator reports that Job continues to bless God (1:21-22), it seems that God's confidence in Job has trumped the Adversary's suspicions.

A second round of the dialogue (2:1-6) begins by repeating almost verbatim the opening exchange. The redundancy serves rhetorically both to reinforce what we readers already know—God has initiated a conversation with the Adversary that triggers an examination of his servant Job—and to up the ante on what is at stake by introducing three new aspects into the conversation (2:3). First, God affirms that Job "still holds on to his integrity" despite what he has experienced. By calling attention to the constancy of Job's virtues (cf. 1:5), God declares that nothing the Adversary has done thus far has altered either Job's fidelity or God's assessment of him. Second, God acknowledges that Job's integrity remains unblemished, "even though you [the Adversary] incited me to ruin him." The verbal construction "incite against" (*sut* + *bĕ*) normally conveys the negative connotation of "provocation," of stirring up someone to an action against another that would not have happened without incitement (e.g., 1 Sam 26:19; 2 Sam 24:1; Jer 43:3). Job 2:3 is the only place in the Hebrew Bible where this expression occurs with God as the object of such incitement. The inference is that God exercises something less than complete sovereignty over divine decisions. Can God be provoked by queries not God's own (or are they?) to do something God would not otherwise have considered?

Third, and still more unsettling, is God's admission that he has yielded to the Adversary's provocation, which results in the innocent deaths of seven sons and three daughters (1:18-19), "for no reason" (*ḥinnām*, 2:3).[10] By (re)inserting (cf. 1:9) these words into God's discourse with the Adversary, the narrator accents the unreasonableness of what God has done. God is an (indirect) agent of gratuitous suffering; there is no reason for Job's animals and servants and children to have died, no rational explanation that can make sense out of what is fundamentally senseless. Inasmuch as the wisdom tradition seeks to attain knowledge and understanding about God and the world by human reasoning, the narrator has used the Joban story to introduce what is perhaps wisdom's most profound challenge to date. Where can wisdom be found, if there is no wisdom to be found?

Seizing on God's admission that there is no rational correlation between human behavior and divine action, the Adversary challenges God once more to extend his hand against Job, this time by permitting him to afflict Job's "bones" and "flesh" (2:5). Once more God accepts the challenge, handing over Job's fate to the Adversary, with a faint, but important caveat: "There he is—within your power; only preserve his life" (2:6). Stepping over the narrative borders between heaven and earth, the Adversary leaves God's presence and steps directly into Job's world. With God's permission he strikes Job with "severe sores from the sole of his foot to the top of his head" (2:7). With these words, God's dialogue with the Adversary comes to an end. The Adversary disappears from the story; in the remainder of the book of Job, he is never mentioned again. God's last words to the Adversary, "he is within your power," mark the last time God will speak until 38:1.

Dialogue, whether real or constructed, is a rhetorical device for the examination of contrasting perspectives and thus a lens through which readers may view the moral values of the characters involved. God's dialogues with the Adversary *invite* such examination, but the narrator *preempts* it. He deflects attention from God and the Adversary by shifting the focus to a conversation between Job and his wife (2:9-10). This conversation he does not hesitate to scrutinize through his own moral lens. Job's wife challenges him to consider whether integrity in the face of senseless suffering requires protest instead of submission; the narrator places his assessment of this thinking on Job's lips: she talks like a "fool." For his part, Job does not question the way God distributes the "good" and the "bad," which is to say, the narrator reminds us—for the second time—Job did not sin (2:10; cf. 1:22).

The prologue construes both the Adversary and Job's wife as negative examples in the sapiential tradition. The Adversary's questions lead only to suffering and death. The wife's challenge to normative thinking is foolish, not wise. Like the primordial couple whom God banishes from the garden for pursuing forbidden knowledge, the narrator, with scribal authority, removes the Adversary and Job's wife from the Edenic world he presents for his readers' consideration.

Ultimate Questions, Penultimate Answers[11]

Questions are essential to the search for knowledge and understanding. They press beyond what can be observed to explore what is hidden from sight, beyond what is known to what has not yet been discovered. The narrator employs questions in the dialogues between God and the Adversary and between Job and his wife, and through these questions readers learn things about these characters that they did not know before. The narrator's last words, however, "In all this, Job didn't sin with his lips" (2:10), envelop the friends and Job as they sit together in silence for seven days and seven nights. The silence temporarily freezes the story and suspends further questions. By God's own admission, what has happened has happened for no reason. Why search for answers that cannot be found?

The poetic dialogues at the center of the book unfreeze the story and resume the questioning. There is no longer a narrator to adjudicate the conversation between Job and the friends, no one to limit the questions that can be asked or to evaluate the answers that may be offered. The wisdom dialogue now moves from the narrator's certainty to the "critical curiosity" of the characters who "live" the Joban story.[12]

On the other side of the prologue's silence, Job's first words are curse and lament. With seven curses—three against the day of his birth (3:3-5) and four against the night of his conception (3:6-9)—Job expresses a death wish. His appropriation of the language and imagery of Genesis 1 suggests he is cursing not only the particular day of his beginnings but also the primordial day of creation that set in motion all beginnings: "God said, 'Let there be light'" (Gen 1:3); "Job said, 'let it be darkness'" (Job 3:4).[13]

In the second half of chapter 3 (vv. 11-26), Job moves from curse to lament. The key word throughout is *Why* (*lāmmâ*, vv. 11, 20; and with different words or by implication in vv. 12, 16, 23). The question is not a mundane query that can be satisfied with a simple answer.[14] Instead, the question is typically directed to God and concerns substantive matters, often with deep implications about life and death, as for example in Job's questions here:

> Why didn't I die at birth,
>> come forth from the womb and die? (v. 11)
>
> Why did knees receive me
>> and breasts let me nurse? . . . (v. 12)

> Why wasn't I like a buried miscarried infant,
> > like babies who never see light? . . . (v. 16)
>
> Why is light given to the hard worker,
> > life to those bitter of soul,
> > those waiting in vain for death,
> > > who search for it more than treasure? . . . (v. 20)
>
> Why is light given to the person whose way is hidden,
> > whom God has fenced in? (v. 23)

Such questions convey protest and accusation that strikes at the heart of cultural orthodoxies. Death is preferable to life, when suffering erases vitality and purpose; better still are those who are never born, for they are spared the disappointment of discovering that life is meaningless.[15] On the one hand, the desire not to have been born is a desire to be free of having to learn hard truths, to be exempt from the futility of all questions, in essence, to remain unknowing, which is the antithesis of wisdom. On the other hand, the precondition for asking such questions is a life of deep thoughtfulness. No young child wonders whether it would have been better not to have been born.[16] The question itself is born of close observation and persistent scrutiny: Why are things as they are? Why is there not more to learn than what is already known? Job presses beyond penultimate maxims to ask ultimate questions about life and death. His questions refuse the silence that descends on the story at the end of the prologue.

Through three cycles of speeches, Job's friends respond to him with questions and answers of their own. In the first cycle (Job 4:4-14), they invite Job to join them in an investigation of God's moral governance of the world, but the questions they pose are rhetorical, not critically inquisitive; they assume answers they believe are unarguable. Eliphaz sets the lead the others will follow.

> Isn't your religion the source of your confidence;
> > the integrity of your conduct, the source of your hope?
>
> Think! What innocent person has ever perished?
> > When have those who do the right thing been destroyed? (4:6-7)

> Does God pervert justice,
>> or does the Almighty distort what is right? (8:3, Bildad)

> Can you find the secret of God
>> or find the extent of the Almighty? (11:7, Zophar)

The friends' questions resolve into propositional truth—a doctrine of retribution grounded in God's revelation to Moses (Deut 30:15-18) and affirmed by the prophets and sages (e.g., Prov 10–15)—that can be attained through "if-then" reasoning: *if* Job will repent, *then* God will forgive the sin that justifies his punishment and bless him with extraordinary prosperity.

> If you are pure and do the right thing,
>> then surely he will become active on your behalf
>> and reward your innocent dwelling.
> Although your former state was ordinary,
>> your future will be extraordinary. (8:6-7, Bildad)

> If you make your mind resolute
>> and spread your palms to him,
> if you throw out the sin in your hands
>> and don't let injustice dwell in your tents,
> then you will lift up your face without blemish;
>> you will be secure and not fear. (11:13-15, Zophar; cf. Eliphaz in 5:8-16)

The second cycle (Job 15–21) generally follows the same pattern as the first. Rhetorical questions (15:2; 18:2; 20:4-5) direct Job to settled truth about divine justice, now focused more narrowly on God's punishment of the guilty than on God's restoration of the righteous (15:17-35; 18:5-21; 20:6-29). Job's continued resistance to the friends' counsel, however, stiffens their resolve to leverage him toward their convictions (15:7-9; 18:3; 20:3). Once again Eliphaz leads the way by accusing Job of crossing the line that divides the wise from the foolish. If Job does not stop his interrogation of God, Eliphaz warns, then he will jeopardize the "fear of God" upon which the entire enterprise of religion rests (15:3; cf.

vv. 9-10). The symmetry of the speeches breaks down in the third cycle (Job 22–27),[17] but it is clear that the friends' questions (22:2-5; 25:4-6) now have a different objective. Having failed to reason Job into agreement with their version of the truth, they render a unilateral decision that ends the pretense of discussion. Job suffers, *therefore* he has sinned (cf. 22:5). Nothing more need be said. Those who contend with God, Bildad says, will learn a truth they did not seek: "Supreme power and awe belong to God," who imposes submission on any and all who contest divine wisdom (25:2; cf. 22:1).

After three rounds of dialogue, the friends have reached a conclusion they believe ends the conversation with Job. Job, however, has resolutely refused their counsel and denied their conclusion. He steadfastly maintains his innocence, insisting that his suffering places God's justice on trial. "I would lay out my case before him," Job says, and "fill my mouth with arguments, know the words with which he would answer, understand what he would say to me" (23:4-5). Job accuses God of abusing divine authority and obstructing justice. He uses three arguments to support his indictment: (1) God has determined "for no reason [*ḥinnām*; cf. 2:3]" that Job is guilty (9:17, 20). Even though there is no "violence" in his hands and his prayer is "pure" (16:17), God crushes him with a savage violence (10:1-7; 16:6-17; 19:6-12; 27:7-12) motivated by hate (16:9). (2) God perverts justice by exonerating the guilty and condemning the innocent (9:22-24; 12:17-25; 21:12-16). Job is an eyewitness to God's corruption (13:1), and he claims that nature itself corroborates his testimony (12:7-9). (3) God has created a world that is morally chaotic. There is no justice because God has created human beings for slavery, not freedom; for harsh, unrewarding labor, not fulfillment, less still for happiness (7:1-6). Like a flower that rises then withers, all mortals come forth from the womb as a shadow that cannot last (14:1-2). The great equalizer in a world that runs amok is death, not God, and even the hope for death is a flawed aspiration, because God sees to it that humans can do no more than stagger toward its mercies like a drunkard groping in the dark (12:25). In sum, Job's arguments return readers to the presenting question in chapter 3, now strategically revised. The question is no longer, "Why didn't *I* die at birth?" (3:11). It has now become an indictment against God: "Why did *you* let me emerge from the womb?" (10:18).

Job wants to "know" (*yādaʿ*) and "understand" (*bîn*) how God would answer him (23:5). He seeks the knowledge and discernment that teachers of wisdom advocate for all their students (Prov 1:2, 4, 7).[18] He is aware that he is asking the impossible—who can summon the creator of the world into court and ask, "What are you doing?" (9:12)—and he assumes he will pay a price for transgressing presumed boundaries between divine wisdom and human knowledge (13:14-15), but he will not desist: "I will say to God, Don't declare me guilty; tell me what [*hôdîʿēnî ʿal mah*, literally, 'make me know why'] you are accusing me of doing?" (10:2).

Impossible questions can sometimes achieve the impossible. The words, "Then the LORD answered Job from the whirlwind" (38:1) introduce the last dialogue in the book. Silent since the prologue, God now steps directly into Job's world and into a conversation with him about matters that both the friends and Job himself must have thought had already been decided (cf. 31:40).[19] Neither in the ancient Near East nor elsewhere in the Old Testament does (any) God enter into direct conversation with someone who demands to know why he is suffering.[20] The general structure and content of this dialogue between God and Job has been outlined above.[21] Here we focus on the two introductions to God's speeches (38:1-2; 40:6-14) and what they disclose about the response from Job that God expects and invites.

The two introductions initiate dialogue about different issues—God's "design" for creation (38:2) and God's "justice" (40:8)—but the form and rhetoric that convey these issues are virtually identical. Three issues invite consideration.

(1) Both introductions couch God's words in poetry, not prose. When God spoke last, it was in the descriptive, matter-of-fact form of a prose narrative. Like the narrator who tells the story, God speaks as a detached observer; he reports objective facts about Job that do not change, even when challenged: "there is no one like him on earth, a man who is honest, who is of absolute integrity, who reveres God and avoids evil" (1:8; 2:3).

Now, God joins the other characters in the story in using the language of poetry, which is more evocative than prose. Its rhetoric is terse and elliptic, suggestive more than descriptive. It does not convey certainties that close discussion; it offers ideas that open the imagination to possibilities not yet considered. In prose, God speaks as one who knows in advance how the story will end; in poetry, God speaks as one whose ideas about endings are not yet finished.

(2) In both introductions, God answers Job "from the whirlwind" (38:1; 40:6). The rhetoric suggests a dialogue that takes place within the context of a theophany. Theophanies mark occasions of divine disclosure, when the holy God approaches the everyday world in extraordinary ways; God comes riding on storm clouds, speaking with a voice that roars like thunder, blazing his way through the earth like lightening (e.g., Ps 18:7-15). Such powerful displays of divine presence evoke dread and fear in those who would contend with God (e.g., Judg 5:4-5; Nah 1:3-6; Hab 3:5-12), and commentators frequently attribute the same purpose to God's words to Job.[22]

Theophanies serve more than one purpose, however. Precisely because they are such awesome, up-close encounters with the holy, they are both frightening and attractive at the same time. On the one hand, people dare not come too close, for the danger is great; on the other, the attraction of such extraordinary proximity to the sacred is so compelling that people instinctively want to come as close possible. The theophany Moses experiences at Sinai is a good example. Standing before a bush that burns without being consumed, Moses hears the voice of God, which both summons him by name ("Moses, Moses!" [Exod 3:4; cf. Exod 19:10-11]) and warns him to be careful ("Don't come any closer! . . . because you are standing on holy ground" [Exod 3:5; cf. Exod 19:12, 21-23]). Moses responds by hiding his face, "because he was afraid to look at God" (Exod 3:6), all the while inching close enough to hear and respond to the mystery that summons him (Exod 3:7-12; cf. Exod 19:17-19).

(3) God's summons to Job recalls God's words to Moses: "Gird up your loins like a man [*geber*], / I will question you [*'eš'ălĕkā*], and you shall declare to me [*hôdî'ēnî*] (38:3 NRSV; 40:7 NRSV). In military terms, a

geber is a "soldier" or "warrior" (Judg 5:30; 2 Sam 23:1) who prepares for battle by tucking the ends of his robe into his belt so that he can run without restriction (2 Sam 20:8; 1 Kgs 2:5; Isa 5:27). Wisdom literature seldom uses the word in this context; however, the maxim in Proverbs 24:5 is instructive: "Stronger a wise man [*geber ḥākām*] than a mighty one, and a man of knowledge [*da ʿat*] than one great in power.²³

God clearly calls Job into a confrontation, but the contest will be waged through the exchange of wisdom and knowledge, not weapons of war. Job had hoped for just such an exchange of ideas with God. He imagined a conventional dialogue in which God would speak and he would answer, or vice versa (13:22; 14:15a). God now invites him into a different kind of dialogue: God will ask questions, Job will convey knowledge to God. The verb for conveying knowledge (*hôdî ʿēnî*, literally, "cause/make me to know") is the same one Job previously used in his request of God: "Tell me [*hôdî ʿēnî*] what you are accusing me of doing" (10:2b; cf. 13:23). Job needed knowledge from God that he could not have unless God gave it to him. God reveals, Job receives; this is the normative process for attaining knowledge that Solomon modeled (1 Kgs 3:5-15) and Israel's sages adopted (cf. Prov 1:1-7). The author of the divine speeches in Job departs from convention. He imagines God asking for and receiving knowledge from Job. It is a stunning depiction of the search for wisdom and understanding that reverses the roles—or at least moderates the difference—between teacher and student.²⁴

Embedded within this shared rhetorical frame are two issues that God invites Job to discuss with him. Both are introduced as questions:

> Who is this darkening counsel
>> with words lacking knowledge? (38:2)

> Would you question my justice,
>> deem me guilty so you can be innocent? (40:8)

The first question—"Who is this?"—is more an expression of God's surprise than an inquiry about the identity of his conversation partner. Who is Job to place a cloud of questions over God's "design" (*ʿēṣâ*; CEB: "counsel") for the world? The word for "design" is used in wisdom literature to describe a plan or a piece of advice that has come about through careful thinking.[25] Job has repeatedly questioned God's design, which seems to him to be chaotic and unjust (see especially 12:13-25). But does Job have the requisite knowledge (*daʿat*) or intellectual capacity to understand what God has done? A litany of additional questions from God ("Have you?" "Can you?" "Do you know?") leads Job to concede the obvious. Job is not God; he did not design the world; he did not create the sun or the moon or any of the creatures that inhabit the world.

> Look, I'm of little worth. What can I answer you?
> I'll put my hand over my mouth.
> I've spoken once, I won't answer,
> twice, I won't do it again. (40:4-5)

If God's objective in the first speech is to invite Job into an exchange of wisdom and knowledge that can only lead to one outcome—the end of deliberation and debate about the way the world works—then Job's silence signals the victory God seeks.

The question in 40:8 indicates that the dialogue with Job is not finished, that God expects and invites something more than Job's silence. God shifts the focus to the issue of divine "justice" (*mišpāṭ*). What capacity does Job have to distinguish between right and wrong? Does he have the requisite judgment to determine who is guilty and who is innocent? More pointedly, would Job "annul" (*tāper*, 40:8; CEB: "question"; cf. 15:4) God's judgment of him? In the prologue, God has affirmed Job's righteousness (1:8; 2:3; cf. 1:1). In the poetic dialogues, Job argues that even though God knows he is "not guilty" (10:7), God nevertheless declares him "perverse" (9:20). Would Job reverse this judgment, declare God guilty of perverting justice by insisting on the integrity of his claim to innocence? The hypothesis—that Job would judge the justice of God—seems implausible by any normative understanding of God's sovereignty (cf. 4:17; 15:14; 25:4).

Nevertheless, God imagines a scenario in which Job's judgment would merit even God's approval. Job would need to exhibit godlike power (40:9a; "an arm like God") and authority (40:9b, "thunder with a voice like him"). He would need to embody the divine qualities of "splendor and majesty" (40:10a); he would need to display the "honor and esteem" of one created by God as "slightly less than divine" (40:10b; cf. Ps 8:5).[26] If Job judged the proud and the wicked with these qualities, if he could bind them up and prevent their diminishment of the moral order, then even God would give thanks for Job's work in the world (40:14).

In the remainder of the second speech, God directs Job's attention to a final pair of animals, Behemoth and Leviathan (40:15–41:34 [Heb. 41:26]). The content of the speech is complex, as one would expect of a "teacher" like God, but the beginning and ending contain a thematic thread. "Look [*hinnēh nā'*]" at Behemoth, God says at the beginning, "Look [*hinnēh nāh'*]" at his strength and power (40:15-16; cf. 12:7). At the conclusion of the speech, the focus is on *looking* at the world through the eyes of Leviathan who, like Behemoth, seems to have qualities that Job shares:

> None on earth can compare to him [Leviathan];
>> he is made to be without fear.
>
> He *looks* [*yir'eh*] on all the proud;[27]
>> he is king over all proud beasts. (41:33-34 [Heb. 41:25-26]; emphasis
>> added)

What is Job supposed to learn from all this looking? What is he supposed to see?

Job's second response to God (42:1-6) conveys his last words in the book. He speaks of what he knows about God's design for the world and concedes that his knowledge is insufficient: "I know [*yāda'tî*] you can do anything . . . I have indeed spoken about things I didn't understand" (42:2-3). He has *heard* what God has said (42:5a). And now he has *seen* (42:5b) God, that is, he has perceived something about God as a result of this encounter that he did not know before. A cognitive shift of some sort has occurred.

The substance of Job's new knowledge is buried in the words of 42:6, which can be translated in such different ways that their meaning exceeds comprehension.[28] Does Job repent or protest? Does he despise himself or

God? Does he retract his previous arguments against God because he now understands that he does not have the standing to make them; that is, he is a mere mortal, no more than "dust and ashes" (cf. 30:19)? Or does he revise his understanding of what it means to be a mere mortal of dust and ashes who, like Abraham (Gen 18:27), dares to stand before God and ask, "Will the judge of all the earth not act justly?" (Gen 18:25).[29]

Job has asked *ultimate* questions about good and evil, justice and injustice, life and death. The friends have offered various answers; Job rejects them all as inadequate and immoral. God has invited Job into an exchange of knowledge about the moral order of the world and about God's governing principles; Job asked that God teach him what he does not know (23:5, "make me know," author's translation); God has asked the same of Job (38:3; 40:7, "make me know," author's translation). When the dialogues end and all the questions have been asked, both Job and his readers are left with penultimate answers. New knowledge has been conveyed and understanding has expanded, but ultimate questions elude closure. One discovery leads to another investigation.

Wisdom, Where Can It Be Found? Where Is the Place of Understanding?

The poem in Job 28 is located at the end of the dialogue between Job and his friends and before the dialogue between Job and God. Whether the poem originated in this location or has been strategically inserted here by a later editor remains a debated question among Job scholars. In either case, its commentary on two models for acquiring wisdom and knowledge—revelation and reason—provides perspective on the book as a whole.[30] The poem divides into three sections (vv. 1-11, 12-19, 20-27). A common refrain introduces sections two and three (vv. 12, 20). Verse 28 provides an interpretive conclusion to the poem. Its summons to learn by seeing calls attention to what humans can (v. 10) and cannot see (v. 21) in relation to what God can see (v. 27). It also annotates Job's new discernment after looking at what God has shown him (42:6).

The poem begins by affirming the extraordinary capacity of human beings to "see" and acquire "everything precious" (v. 10). With exquisite images of a miner seeking precious gems and metals, the author provides a paradigm for reflecting on the search for wisdom, which the sages consider more valuable than gold and silver (Prov 16:16; cf. 8:10-11; 20:15). Zophar chided Job about his limitations, "Can you find the limit [*taklît*; CEB: 'extent'] of the Almighty?" (11:7 NRSV). Normative wisdom imagines only one possible answer to the question, "No." Considering the work of miners, however, opens the imagination and expands the horizons of possibilities.[31] Miners have both the courage and the capacity to reach the farthest limit (*taklît*, 28:3; CEB: "depths") of what is humanly possible. They can cut and carve their way through almost every obstacle until they come right to the edge of the mysteries God alone oversees. They open shafts (v. 4) and dig out channels (v. 10). They overturn mountains as if pulling them up by their roots (v. 9) and dam up the subterranean sources of rivers (v. 11a). All this they must do in isolation, for they work in remote places where ordinary people never go (v. 4b), places the sharp-eyed hawk cannot see (v. 7), places the lion, the most courageous of all animals, has not prowled (v. 8). They can "put an end to darkness" (v. 3) and bring into the light things once hidden (v. 11b), and in doing so they come as close to the ultimate prize—wisdom and understanding like that which God possesses—as humans can get (cf. 12:13, 22).

The second section (vv. 12-19) makes clear, however, that wisdom and understanding are not material objects like silver and gold. They do not reside in a place that a miner's tool can uncover. Proverbs 8 personifies Wisdom, stations her at the entrance to the city, and makes her accessible to everyone: "those who seek me will find me" (8:17). In a remarkable reversal of this image, Job 28 personifies the Deep (v. 14a), the Sea (v. 14b), Destruction, and Death (v. 22) and has each one declare that they have no idea where wisdom can be found. Its source is not in any place on earth. It cannot be excavated with human ingenuity, and it cannot be acquired through second-hand commercial transactions. A skillful person might acquire every precious gem that exists in the world—gold, silver, onyx, lapis lazuli, coral, jasper, rubies, and topaz—but not one of these would have sufficient value to purchase wisdom (vv. 15-19). The question that begins the section remains unanswered: "Wisdom, where can it be found; where is the place of understanding?" (v. 12).

Verse 20 introduces the third section with essentially the same question and proceeds to answer it, although in a way that stretches normative wisdom's understanding. Humans do not know and cannot find the place (*maqôm*, v. 12) of wisdom, but God "knows her place [*měqômâ*]" (v. 23). Humans can see and seize penultimate treasures (v. 10), but wisdom and understanding are hidden from all eyes (v. 21) but God's. As creator, God "looks to the ends of the earth" and sees everything "beneath the heavens" (v. 24). God, and God alone, can see the whole and then reveal it to humans by saying, "Look," this is wisdom (v. 28a). The issue for the author of Job 28, however, is not how far God sees but instead how God obtains and exercises wisdom.

The focus shifts to reflection on four specific aspects of God's work as creator (vv. 25-27). God made the wind and fixed its proper weight in the balance of earth's forces. God made the primordial waters and carefully measured their place in the world. God made the rain and set a limit on the amount of water that would fall on earth. God made the thunderbolt and plotted the way for its travel. The grammar of these verses indicates that it is "in the act of" (*laʿăśôt*, v. 25; *baʿăśotô*, v. 26) engaging these forces and determining their role in the world that God obtains wisdom. Some English translations capture this sense nicely by rendering verses 25 and 26 as subordinate clauses that introduce the main clause in verse 27: "*When* he gave to the wind its weight . . . *when* he made a decree for the rain . . . *then* he saw it and declared it; he established it, and searched it out" (NRSV; NJPS; NEB). The implication is that wisdom is not something *in* God, something God possesses *before* God creates the world. It is instead something God *acquires* in the very act of creative engagement with the world. A part of the answer to the question, "Wisdom, where can it be found?" now clarifies. Wisdom is not found in any spatial location. It comes from creatively interacting with the world, that is, from weighing, measuring, setting limits, and charting courses that offer the best possibilities for the world to become all that God intends.

A close reading of the verbs in verse 27 clarifies another significant part of the answer. The four verbs—"observed" (*rā'āh*), "appraised" (*sāpar*; CEB: "spoke"), "established" (*kûn*), and "searched" (*ḥqr*)—are generic and may be used to describe both divine and human activity.[32] The root word for "search" (*ḥqr*) is particularly instructive. The motif of searching, exploring, or investigating a matter in order to comprehend it fully occurs frequently in Job. Both the friends (5:9; 36:26; cf. 11:7) and Job (9:10) concede that some things, especially the ways of God, are "unsearchable" (*'ēn / lō' ḥēqer*). Even so, both the friends (5:27) and Job (29:16; CEB: "the case I didn't know, I examined") remain fully engaged in a process of intense exploration. Of all the places this motif occurs in Job, none is more suggestive than the references in chapter 28 to the search for wisdom. According to 28:3, miners have a God-like capacity to search (*ḥqr*) the farthest boundaries of their world in pursuit of its most precious and hidden treasures. Although they cannot obtain every treasure, they work in ways that approximate what God can do. The pursuit of ultimate treasures—we may decode the metaphor, ultimate wisdom—leads to extraordinary penultimate discoveries. The *miner's God-like capacity* and *God's human-like capacity* are near mirror images of the same search. As one commentator observes, "Transcendent wisdom and human wisdom are in some sense continuous after all."[33]

Verse 28 resolves the question about the search for wisdom into the final part of its answer: wisdom is "fear of the LORD" that is manifest in ethical behavior, that is, in "turning from evil." The answer appears to return the story rather simplistically back to its beginnings. The prologue stipulates that fearing God and avoiding evil are the qualities Job exemplified (1:1, 8; 2:3) *before* he filled his mouth with questions and arguments, *before* he critically examined received truth and discovered that its axioms are made of ashes and its answers are made of clay (13:12). On first inspection, the author who inserted Job 28 into the story seems to have sided with the friends (and with the sage who advocates the "fear of the LORD" in Prov 1–9) and against Job: the true measure of wisdom is piety, not protest, receiving whatever God gives—both the good and the bad—without asking why. This assessment would not only validate the friends, but also elucidate Job's ambiguous last words in 42:5-6. After his encounter with God, Job saw and comprehended more than he had before: true wisdom always exceeds the grasp of human intelligence. Having learned his lesson, therefore, Job takes comfort in the dust and ashes of normative wisdom, superficial though its discernments may be.

Even normative wisdom recognizes, however, that "sound insight has two sides" (11:6). The contrast between God's wisdom and human wisdom provides context for understanding the limitations of human reasoning, but it does not minimize the importance of searching for truth that eludes discovery. Even if the difference between what God knows and what humans can understand can never be closed, the desire to see what is hidden, to discover something yet unknown expands the limits of what is possible. The supreme model of such a search and discovery process is God himself. "Look how I found wisdom," God says (or the sage says through God). "I observed, appraised, established, and searched to the ends of heaven and earth." To engage in such an intellectual process is the epitome of piety, not its antithesis, as the friends suggest (15:4). It is the path toward wisdom acquired through the moral habit of resisting evil.[34]

On the heels of this poem, Job takes up his subject again in chapters 29–31. Once again he defends his integrity, weighs his innocence against assumptions about his guilt, ponders the disconnect between his moral rectitude and God's justice, and resolves to continue his search for truth that he cannot as yet attain. If this is what it means to fear God and avoid evil, then the sage responsible for the commentary in Job 28 may be signaling that it is Job who transforms prologue piety rather than the other way around.

Epilogue or Eulogy?

An epilogue (*epilogus*) is an additional word that brings a story to a conclusion. In the final form of the book of Job, the narrator (re)appears and offers two judgments meant to bring the Joban drama to a coherent and satisfying ending. The first (42:7-9) is God's judgment *against* the friends, who "haven't spoken about me correctly"; the second (42:10-17) is God's judgment *for* Job, which results in the restoration of his wealth, family, and place in society. This story (omitting the poetic dialogues in the center of the book) is a narrative version of proverbial wisdom:

> Don't let loyalty and faithfulness leave you.
>> Bind them on your neck;
>>> write them on the tablet of your heart.
>
> Then you will find favor and approval
>> in the eyes of God and humanity.
>
> Trust in the Lord with all your heart;
>> don't rely on your own intelligence. . . .
>
> Don't consider yourself wise.
>> Fear the Lord and turn away from evil.
>
> Then your body will be healthy
>> and your bones strengthened. . . .
>
> The Lord loves those he corrects,
>> just like a father who treats his son with favor. (Prov 3:3-5, 7-8, 12)

The final form of the book of Job, however, complicates reading it as a tidy all's-well-that-ends-well story. Whether this final form is the accidental product of multiple redactors or the skillful work of a single author, 42:7-17 now represents the conclusion to the *whole* story. One must read *from* the prologue, then *through* the middle section of Job's dialogues with the friends and with God, *in order to arrive at whatever conclusion* the epilogue offers. When the book is read straight through from beginning to end, the narrator's conclusion is no longer simple.[35]

The narrator dismisses the friends as incorrect, but does this mean he also dismisses the conventional wisdom they espouse? If so, why does the epilogue essentially affirm their errant doctrine by affirming that the righteous actually do prosper, just as the friends had argued? If Job has spoken correctly about God, then do all of his words merit this evaluation or only some of them? Does Job speak truth only when he blesses God and humbly submits to God's inscrutable wisdom? Or, does he also speak truthfully by relentlessly pursuing knowledge that conventional wisdom would deny him? Does his encounter with God lead him to subordinate human reasoning to divine revelation? Or, does it expand the horizon for probing the unknown by revealing that he imitates God when he does?

Job 28 provides commentary on the book as a whole by comparing and contrasting human wisdom and transcendent wisdom. It not only rereads prologue piety but also exegetes the last words of the friends, Job, God, and the narrator. Yet even as Job 28 hints that a robust intellectual pursuit of wisdom is the essence of fidelity to God, the immediately following chapters mitigate the lesson by returning to a story that reifies Job's silent submission to God's autocracy.

An epilogue is a coda, an additional and potentially finalizing word. The last words of the Joban epilogue read like a eulogy: "After this, Job lived 140 years and saw four generations of his children. Then Job died, old and satisfied" (42:16-17). Eulogies normally signify that a person's death merits recognition, and this is certainly the intention of the last words in the Joban story. But this eulogy, like wisdom itself, invites close scrutiny. What dies with Job is not only the celebration of his piety but also the relentless interrogative spirit that his story briefly contributed to the sapiential tradition. Qohelet will excavate and sustain aspects of Job's discontent with normative wisdom, but wisdom's more orthodox representatives, past (Proverbs) and future (Sirach and Wisdom of Solomon), will ultimately muffle his voice, just like Job's. The book of Job ends with a simple declaration of Job's death. The question that lurks just beneath the surface is this: Does the death of Joban dissonance represent a development within Israel's wisdom tradition to be celebrated or mourned?

For Further Reading

Balentine, S. E. *Have You Considered My Servant Job: Understanding the Biblical Archetype of Patience.* Columbia: University of South Carolina Press, 2015.

Bloom, H. *Where Shall Wisdom Be Found?* New York: Chelsea House, 1998.

Boss, J. *Human Consciousness of God in the Book of Job: A Theological and Psychological Commentary.* New York: T & T Clark, 2010.

Doak, B. *Consider Leviathan: Narratives of Nature and Self in Job.* Minneapolis, MN: Fortress, 2014.

Habel, N. *Finding Wisdom in Nature: An Eco-Wisdom Reading of the Book of Job.* Sheffield, UK: Sheffield Phoenix, 2014.

Hankins, D. *The Book of Job and the Immanent Genesis of Transcendence.* Evanston, IL: Northwestern University Press, 2015.

Hoffman, Y. *A Blemished Perfection: The Book of Job in Context.* Sheffield, UK: Sheffield Academic Press, 1996.

Janzen, J. G. *At the Scent of Water: The Ground of Hope in the Book of Job.* Grand Rapids, MI: William B. Eerdmans, 2009.

Kynes, W. *My Psalm Has Turned into Weeping.* BZAW 437. Berlin: Walter de Gruyter, 2012.

Larrimore, M. *The Book of Job: A Biography.* Princeton, NJ: Princeton University Press, 2013.

Low, K. *The Bible, Gender, and Reception History: The Case of Job's Wife.* London: Bloomsbury T & T Clark, 2013.

Mathewson, D. *Death and Survival in the Book of Job: Desymbolization and Traumatic Experience.* New York: T & T Clark, 2006.

Nelson, A. J. *Power and Responsibility in Biblical Interpretation: Reading the Book of Job with Edward Said.* Sheffield, UK: Equinox, 2012.

Newsom, C. *The Book of Job: A Contest of Moral Imaginations.* Oxford: Oxford University Press, 2003.

Pelham, A. *Contested Creations in the Book of Job: The-World-as-It-Ought-to-Be and Ought-Not-to-Be.* Leiden: Brill, 2012.

Schifferdecker, K. *Out of the Whirlwind: Creation Theology in the Book of Job.* Cambridge, MA: Harvard University Press, 2008.

Terrien, S. *The Iconography of Job through the Centuries: Artists as Biblical Interpreters.* University Park: The Pennsylvania State University Press, 1996.

Tollerton, D. C. *The Book of Job in Post-Holocaust Thought.* Bible in the Modern World 44. Sheffield, UK: Sheffield Phoenix, 2012.

Van Wolde, E. ed. *Job 28: Cognition in Context.* Leiden: Brill, 2003.

Zuckerman, B. *Job the Silent: A Study in Historical Counterpoint.* New York: Oxford University Press, 1991.

Chapter 3

Ecclesiastes

"Perfectly Pointless"

Job and Ecclesiastes are dissonant voices in Israelite wisdom literature. When the author of the prose introduction looks on the collapse of Job's world—the loss of his possessions, the death of his children, the personal affliction that assaults his integrity—he concludes that there is no rational explanation for what one experiences in life. A capricious God deals out the "good" and the "bad," reward and punishment, "for no reason" (*ḥinnām*, 2:3), evoking wounded submission from the righteous and appalled silence from friends who would comfort them. When Qohelet (the "Teacher of the Assembly") looks on his world, he concludes that "everything" he sees, the entirety of human existence, is "perfectly pointless" (*hăbēl hăbālîm hakkōl hābel*, Eccl 1:2). What happens to the fool indiscriminately befalls the righteous as well. Irrespective of guilt and innocence, the same fate happens to all (Eccl 2:14).

Israelite sages, like intellectuals in all times and places, make it their business to understand and explain the world as best they can. The authors of Proverbs, Sirach, and the Wisdom of Solomon essentially agree that God creates and consistently enforces a universal moral order of cause and effect. They attribute experiences that exceed human understanding to the inscrutable wisdom of God. There is no cause to question what one does not understand, no reason to protest or complain that one ought to know more. Instead, there is a calm recognition that the one who trusts God is safe and secure (e.g., Prov 14:26; 16:3, 20; 18:10; 29:25; Wis 1:2; 3:9; Sir 1:13; 2:6).

Job and Qohelet are not persuaded. In different ways, both press the wisdom tradition to its limits. Job's beleaguered affirmation—"Naked I came from my mother's womb; naked I will return there. The LORD has given; the LORD has taken; bless the LORD's name" (Job 1:21)—is for Qohelet a pointless and "sickening tragedy" (Eccl 6:2). Those "who have already died, are more fortunate than the living," Qohelet concludes; "happier than both are those who have never existed, who haven't witnessed the terrible things that happen under the sun" (Eccl 4:2-3). This grim perspective on life would seem to link Qohelet more with the pessimism of the French existentialist Jean-Paul Sartre (1905–80) than with the proverbial wisdom of Solomon.[1] An observation from a distinguished wisdom scholar of a previous generation is still apt:

> Ecclesiastes is the strangest book in the Bible, or at any rate the book whose presence in the sacred canons of Judaism and Christianity is most inexplicable. . . . It diverges too radically [with the rest of the Bible]. In fact, it denies some of the things on which other writers lay the greatest stress—notably that God has revealed himself and his will to man, through his chosen people Israel. In Ecclesiastes God is not only unknown to man through revelation; he is unknowable through reason, the only means by which the author believes knowledge is attainable. Such a God is not Yahweh, the covenant God of Israel.[2]

Authorship, Date, and Structure

The search for answers to conventional introductory questions about the book of Ecclesiastes—authorship, date, setting, and form—confronts interpreters with a number of problems at the very outset. The initial verse ascribes authorship to "Qohelet; CEB: "Teacher of the Assembly", David's son, king in Jerusalem" (author's translation). David did not have a son named Qohelet, however, so we must reckon from the beginning with a literary fiction that invites hearing these words *as if* they convey a royal perspective. The royal perspective itself seems only an experiment;

the author employs it briefly in 1:12–2:11, then abandons it throughout the rest of the book for introspective, autobiographical speech based on personal experience, not traditional authority ("I have seen/observed").[3] The fiction is reinforced and complicated by the seven occurrences of the word "Qohelet" throughout the book, as a personal name (1:1, 2, 12), with the definite article, thus as a reference to one's title or function (7:27; 12:8), and as a legendary sage who studied and taught wisdom (12:9, 10). The noun, a feminine participle from the verb *qāhal*, "to convoke, assemble," refers to someone who collects wisdom sayings and by extension, to a "speaker" (REB), "teacher" (NRSV, NIB, CEB), or "preacher" (Luther: *Prediger*; cf. the LXX title for the book, "Ekklesiastes," "one who leads a congregation [*ekklesia*]"). Jerusalem may be the geographical locus of the author, but Qohelet's Hebrew, which includes Aramaic and occasional Persian loanwords, suggests a date not in the Solomonic period but instead in the late Persian or, more likely, Ptolemaic period, circa 250 BCE.

Apart from oblique statements about Qohelet, there is no verifiable information about the identity of the author. Moreover, changing voices in the book convey different and often inconsistent perspectives. In the framing narrative (1:1-2; 12:8-12), an anonymous reader and interpreter of the text refers to Qohelet in the third person. Speaking as one who knows the beginning and ending of the "book," he introduces its principal theme— "Perfectly pointless . . . perfectly pointless. Everything is pointless" (1:2)— and offers a summation of its purpose, which is to goad readers to heed the words of the wise, even if they are painful to hear: "The words of the wise are like iron-tipped prods . . . like nails fixed firmly by a shepherd" (12:11).

Inside this framing narrative, we hear the voice of Qohelet, or someone assuming the persona (mask) of Qohelet, speaking in first-person (1:3–12:7). Two poems bracket a central message. The first poem (1:3-11) is a reflection on the futility of life; the second (12:1-7), on the inevitability of death. Sandwiched between these poems are two discourses on the predicament of life. The first (1:12–6:9) picks up the motto in 1:2 and develops it with a refrain that repeats seven times with some variation, "everything is pointless, a chasing after wind" (1:14; 2:11, 17, 26; 4:4, 16; 6:9). The second, 6:10–11:10, extends Qohelet's search for what is "good" in life (*ṭôb*, 2:3; CEB:

"worth"; cf. 6:12) with another set of refrains, "can't discover"/"can't find," "can't grasp," "don't know" (6:10; 7:14, 27; 8:7, 17; 9:1, 10; 10:14; 11:2, 5, 6). Other refrains occur throughout the book, none more structurally or theologically decisive than the statement, "There's nothing better for human beings than to eat, drink, and experience pleasure in their hard work," which repeats with some variation seven times (2:24-26; 3:12-13, 22; 5:18-20 [Heb. 17-19]; 8:14-15; 9:7-10; 11:7–12:1).

The perspectives conveyed in the frame narrative (1:1-2; 12:8-12) and the first-person accounts (1:3–12:7) are essentially in concord. The frame is likely editorial, but not necessarily from a different author. The final verses (12:13-14) introduce ideas not found elsewhere in the book, a call to keep God's commandments and an allusion to eschatological judgment, which come from a later editor who thought a pious, more orthodox, ending was needed.

Ecclesiastes

1:1-2 Introduction with thematic statement: "Perfectly pointless, says the Teacher, perfectly pointless. Every-thing is pointless."

1:3-11 Opening poem on the futility of life

1:12–6:9 Life is "pointless, a chasing after wind" (1:14, also 1:17; 2:11, 17, 26; 4:4, 6, 16; 6:9)

6:10–11:10 "Who knows what's good for human beings during life?" (6:12); note the refrains "can't discover"/"can't find" (7:14, 27), "can't grasp" (8:7, 17), "don't know" (9:1, cf. 9:10; 10:14; 11:2, 5)

12:1-7 Closing poem on the inevitability of death

12:8-12 Conclusion with thematic statement: "Perfectly pointless, says the Teacher, everything is pointless" (12:8)

12:13-14 Appendix

Rhetorical Strategy

This general outline illustrates the rhetorical strategy of the book, the repetition of key words and phrases that signal central themes in Qohelet's teaching. The thematic statement in 1:2, "Everything is pointless," announces the horizon of the sage's concerns. The word "everything" (*kōl*) occurs ninety-one times in Ecclesiastes[4], an indicator that Qohelet's objective is to explore the totality of life, everything that happens "under the sun," a phrase that repeats twenty-nine times. It is a pursuit of knowledge and understanding about human existence that exceeds anything else in Israel's wisdom tradition. Even God, whose domain is "in heaven" (5:2 [Heb. 5:1]), and whose ways defy all human understanding (11:5), is subject to Qohelet's intellectual inquiries. Among the various subjects to which Qohelet returns again and again, the following deserve special attention.

"Pointless" (hebel)

This noun, which provides a thematic refrain for the book (1:2; 12:8), occurs thirty-eight times, roughly 60 percent of the total occurrences of the word in the Hebrew Bible. A wide range of translations is possible, including "meaningless," "futile," "absurd," "incomprehensible," "delusion," "enigmatic," and the conventional "vanity" (NRSV, NKJV, NAB). A base line for all translations is the literal meaning "vapor/breath," which Qohelet uses as a metaphor for something that is ephemeral, present one moment but gone the next, in short something both too impermanent and too unreliable to give meaning to life. Even if one has the unlimited resources of a king, as Qohelet claims for himself in 2:1-11, and is able to build houses, plant vineyards, and acquire wealth that exceeds all others, his legacy will not last; among the living "there is no eternal memory of the wise any more than the foolish, because everyone is forgotten before long" (2:16). Toil and labor produce riches, but the gain is erased when one dies, for the wealth will be left to someone else, who may be more foolish than wise (2:17-18; cf. 3:9; 5:10-17; 6:1-9). Companionship adds pleasure and security to life, but it does not prevent anyone from needing help, for there is always trouble lurking somewhere (4:7-12). "A three-ply cord doesn't *easily* snap" (4:12b), but when adversity comes, it is the qualifying adverb that hints of the weak link in the chain. Life is better than death, so one should seize the day, but because "everything is pointless— just wind chasing," there will be times to "hate" life rather than enjoy it (2:17), times when those "who have already died, are more fortunate than the living" (4:2), times when "chance" stops humans in their tracks, like fish caught in a net or birds in a trap (9:11-12).

As the examples above illustrate, the word *hebel* typically has negative inferences. To declare something *hebel* is to associate it with "madness" (2:2), "a terrible wrong" (2:21), "pain" and "aggravation" (2:23), "a terrible obsession" (4:8), and "a sickening tragedy" (6:2). What is tragic about the pointlessness of human existence, Qohelet observes, is that there is nothing one can do either to change the circumstances of life or to understand them. There is an unremitting tension between what is and what ought to be, a disconnect between expectation and reality. When everything is "perfectly pointless," as the narrator declares with the use of the superlative in 1:2 (*hăbēl hăbālîm*), there is no reason to complain or protest, no reason to hope for change, and no reason to think about why there are no reasons to be found for "what God has done from beginning to end" (3:11). Qohelet's observations strike at the foundations of the wisdom enterprise. Why aspire to be wise—or just or righteous or virtuous—if everything, wisdom included, is as pointless as chasing the wind?

"Fate, Chance" (miqreh; CEB: "accidents")

Seven of the ten occurrences of this noun in the Old Testament are in Ecclesiastes (2:14, 15; 3:19 [three times]; 9:2, 3; cf. verbal forms in 2:14, 15; 9:11). Outside this book, the word has a positive (unexpected good luck, Ruth 2:3) or neutral connotation (Deut 23:10 [Heb. 23:11]; 1 Sam 6:9; 20:26), but Qohelet typically uses it to convey a negative assessment of wisdom's capacity to determine or even influence what happens in life. Things happen to people over which they have no control. It is impossible to know in advance what will occur, hence it matters little what one does.

It is better to be wise than foolish, even if wisdom is always "elusive and utterly unfathomable" (7:24; cf. 8:16-17), but if ultimately what happens to one happens also to the other, then why expend the effort (2:15)? One may assume that humans have some intellectual advantage over animals, that they can think their way through to longer, more fulfilling lives, either in this world or the next, but "who knows if a human being's life-breath rises upward while an animal's life-breath descends into the earth?" The only certain lesson life teaches is that "all go to the same place: all are from the dust; all return to the dust" (3:20-21).

It is better to be righteous than wicked, but the same fate comes to both (9:2-3). If one's behavior has no bearing on the way God treats people, then is not indifference to piety and ethics the prudent path to follow? Qohelet counsels a middle course: "Don't be too righteous or too wise, or you may be dumfounded" (7:16). Chance, not choice, determines what happens in life, Qohelet says; "this is the sad thing about all that happens under the sun: the same fate awaits everyone." Until death, the ultimate and unavoidable fate, lays its claim on all people, their "minds are full of madness while they are alive" (9:3).

Death

Qohelet uses conventional Hebrew vocabulary for death, and there is nothing exceptional about the number of occurrences of specific terms.[5] Nonetheless, this sage is preoccupied with the general topic of death in a way not found in the older wisdom literature of Proverbs.[6] Following the prologue (1:1-2), Qohelet introduces and frames all of his observations with two poems about the utter pointlessness of life (1:3-11) and the absolute inescapability of death (12:1-7). A question begins the first poem, "What do people gain from all the hard work that they work so hard at under the sun?" (1:3). Does anything one accomplishes have an impact on the way the world works? Does anything one achieves in the course of a lifetime add to the quality of one's life? The question is merely rhetorical; the answer, which Qohelet defers until 2:11—hard work makes absolutely no difference—is a given. The world remains unchanged, whatever the sun, wind, and sea may contribute to its upkeep (1:4-7); life is not improved nor is one's understanding enlarged, despite what may be accomplished through speech, sight, and hearing (1:8-11). *Everything* that happens "under the sun," in the realm of the living, is pointless.

The second poem (12:1-7) uses a range of images to demonstrate that a pointless life inexorably ends in a pointless death. The descent into nothingness begins in one's youth, before any signs of the diminishment of life that is to come are even thinkable. Slowly but surely strength yields to weakness and suffering; labor ceases, panic and fear of what is coming next take hold. A sequence of vivid verbs describes the last steps of the journey to the grave, "smashed" (CEB: "snaps"), "shattered," "broken," "crushed" (12:6). At the beginning of life and at the end of death, the verdict is the same, "perfectly pointless, says the Teacher, . . . everything is pointless" (1:2; cf. 12:8).[7]

Inside these two framing poems, the specter of death hangs like the sword of Damocles over nearly every aspect of Qohelet's thinking. "There's a season for everything," the sage says, including birth and death, but no one can decide when such events occur; they can only respond to them when they do (3:1-8). The wise and the righteous may have some advantage in life over fools, they may be able to discern the best time to speak persuasively or to act decisively (Prov 15:23; 25:11; cf. Sir 1:23-24; 4:20, 23), but only God knows when a person's breathing will end (8:8), and, apparently, premature death may interfere even with God's plan (7:17; cf. Job 22:16). It is better, ideally, to be alive than to be dead, but in reality people have no choice in the matter. They live until they die, and they can do nothing to extend their expiration date. They die when they cease to live, leaving behind no evidence that they ever drew a breath (9:4-5).

Not only is death inevitable; it is also indiscriminate. Covenantal theology offers people a clear choice: "Today I've set before you life and what's good versus death and what's wrong. If you obey the LORD your God's commandments . . . then you will live and thrive. . . . But if your heart turns away and you refuse to listen . . . you will definitely die. . . . Now choose life—so that you and your descendants will live" (Deut 30:15-19). Proverbs embraces this theology by causally connecting life with wisdom and righteous behavior, death with folly and wickedness (e.g., Prov 5:22-23; 10:27; 11:30-31; 12:7, and often). Qohelet, however, does not see any moral distinction between right and wrong, no connection between how one lives and how one dies. God, the world, and nature itself are completely indifferent to human existence. Neither one's death nor one's life has any ultimate meaning, which begs a destabilizing question from any sage who seeks to understand how the world works: "Who knows what's good for human beings during life, during their brief pointless life, which will pass away like a shadow? Who can say what the future holds for people under the sun?" (6:12). As in 1:3 (cf. 2:22; 3:9), the question is only rhetorical; the answer is already certain: "No one."

"Enjoyment, Pleasure" (śimḥâ)

In a text in which the Teacher's first words are "perfectly pointless," it is at the very least curious to find substantive instruction on how to enjoy life. Qohelet uses the term in the seven *carpe diem* ("seize the day") refrains that provide the leitmotif of the book (2:24-26; 3:12-13, 22; 5:18-20 [Heb. 5:17-19]; 8:15; 9:7-9; 11:7-10).[8] He identifies the potential for pleasure in four things: labor, eating and drinking, love, and youth. He examines the joy that people may create for themselves out of their own resources by building, planting, and acquiring possessions, but he concludes that these things are "of no use at all" (2:2). He commends instead the simple pleasures of life, eating and drinking, essential aspects of conviviality and pleasure that have nothing to do with earned gain or profit (2:24; 3:13, 22; 5:18; 8:15). Sufficient bread, wine, clothes, and oil make life worth living. Having someone to love increases joy by adding companionship for "all the days of your pointless life!" (9:9). Old age, harbinger of death, stalks life relentlessly, grinding away at every joy God grants; so the time to maximize pleasure is when one is young and the consequences for following "your heart's inclinations and whatever your eyes see" seem too distant to matter (11:9).

Qohelet's commendation of pleasure invites different assessments. On the one hand, he advocates joy as a gift, not an achievement, a perspective

71

that frees one to enjoy the moment, to work, love, and live fully and without reservation in the present, irrespective of what may come next. On the other, he concedes that the gift of joy may be no more than an anesthetic that dulls the pain of life but does not remove it. One interpretation tilts toward the "mysteriously incidental quality" of God's providence, which cannot be understood but should be trusted,[9] the other toward the concession that God teases humans with ephemeral joy only to afflict them with permanent pain.[10]

Either assessment invites reflection on the ethics of the joy Qohelet commends. The mystery of divine providence may evoke awe and wonder.[11] Faced with the incomprehensibility of divine wisdom, human beings may acknowledge their limitations and bow in reverential submission to the God they willingly trust with their lives. They aspire not to change or correct the world God has created but instead to enjoy its small comforts. The ethics of *awed* joy lead to a transformation in one's attitude about life, but they do not necessarily require a change in behavior that effects social transformation.[12] People should not be indifferent to the poor and needy (4:9-12; 11:1-2), but they can learn to look beyond human misery, beyond injustice, poverty, and suffering, in order to celebrate serendipitous good fortune. No one can "straighten what God has made crooked," Qohelet concludes. "When times are good, enjoy the good; when times are bad, consider: God has made the former as well as the latter" (7:13-14).

But joy conferred by the mystery of divine providence may also produce a different ethic. If by design joy is fleeting and distress is permanent, then awe and wonder may become shock and terror. If living seems always to result in being victimized by unscrupulous and irresistible power, then the ethics of *awed* joy may perforce become an ethics of *terrorized compliance* to regnant control. What cannot be known no longer provides incentive to rely on gratuitous benevolence; it is a cause to cower before unpredictable malice. The tease of ephemeral joy is the summons to accept a life without options or choices. "Whatever happens has already been designated," Qohelet observes, and humans "can't contend with the one who is stronger than they are" (6:10; cf. Job 15:1-3; 22:21-22; 34:36-37; 36:22-23). There may be nothing "good" ('ên ṭôb, 2:24; 3:12, 22; 8:15) under the sun except to eat, drink, and enjoy life, but to try to make sense of the moral and ethical aspects of this assessment—and of "the God" who is implicated by them—is a "bad business," even for a sage (*'inyān rā'*, 1:13; 4:8; CEB: "unhappy/terrible obsession").

"[The] God" ([hā]'ĕlōhîm)

Qohelet always uses the generic word *'ĕlōhîm* for God (forty times), over half of the occurrences with the definite article, "the God."[13] This designation betrays a distance between Qohelet and the God he experiences as hidden behind an impenetrable veil of secrecy. He acknowledges that God "gives" (*nātan*; 1:13; 2:26; 3:10, 11; 5:18-19; 6:2; 8:15; 9:9; 12:7) wisdom, knowledge, work, wealth, possessions, joy, love, and life itself; that God "makes" (*'āśâ*; 3:11, 14; 7:14, 29; 8:17; 11:5) everything in the world the way it is, with the caveat that no one can understand what God is doing or why. Qohelet's God remains nonetheless wholly transcendent. Unlike Proverbs, Qohelet does not personify Wisdom as God's agent on earth (e.g., Prov 8); instead, he accents the unbridgeable distance between God and human beings: "God is in heaven, but you are on earth" (5:2; contrast Deut 4:39). Between heaven and earth there is a void. God does not speak, does not extend a hand to help, does not make covenant promises to be present, does not reveal either a divine plan or purpose for anything or anyone on earth. On the other side of this divine-human chasm, Qohelet never prays, sacrifices, or makes vows to "the God," and he commends caution to those who do: "Watch your steps when you go to God's house. It's more acceptable to listen than to offer the fools' sacrifice" (5:1). Any word spoken to "the God" risks retaliation. Whatever good intentions may have motivated address, God may become angry and destructive (5:6). As one commentator puts it, "God and mortals do not belong in the same realms."[14]

The hidden God is nonetheless palpably present to Qohelet. Denied full comprehension of the divine, he understands that God has placed a sense of the whole within the human heart (3:11). The "memory of transcendence,"[15] an elusive but abiding image of what is eternal, enables finite human beings to imagine infinity but not to understand what it means. It is not only the gift of joy that is ephemeral, it is also the very conception of divinity; as soon as the human mind makes it thinkable, it becomes unthinkable. Humans must therefore learn to be satisfied with the "portion" (*ḥēleq*, 2:10, 21; 3:22; 5:17, 18; 9:6, 9) of the whole God has given them. Such learning effectively puts one on a path toward intellectual nihilism. The pursuit of knowledge is a wearying "task" (*'inyān*) that is not only associated with "bad business" (*'inyān rā'*, 1:13; 4:8; CEB: "unhappy/terrible obsession") but also with the utter futility of the entire wisdom enterprise: "I set my mind to know wisdom [*ḥokmâ*] and to observe the business ['*inyān*] that happens on earth. . . . I observed all the work of God—that no one can grasp what happens under the sun. Those who strive to know can't grasp it. Even the wise who are set on knowing are unable to grasp it" (8:16-17).

Does Qohelet believe that God intends the collapse of the human quest for knowledge and wisdom, and if so, what would be God's rationale for effecting such a failure? Qohelet, and the wisdom tradition in general, assumes that God created and sustains a moral order in which actions have appropriate consequences. Good deeds produce good results; bad deeds, bad results. By understanding this cause-and-effect moral system, the sages are able to explain life's ebbs and flows. They can discern a reasonable cause for everything that happens. *If* there is misfortune, *then* its cause can be identified, corrected, and eliminated through divine intervention or human agency. A moral equilibrium can be restored; chaos and confusion can be averted, or at least curtailed. By the same logic, Qohelet observes, *if* there is no such moral system, *if* there are no obtainable reasons or explanations for what happens in life, *then* everything is "perfectly pointless." God does what God does "for no reason," an assessment the Joban narrator attributes to God himself (Job 2:3). Humans have no moral agency; they can neither understand God's decisions through intellectual inquiry nor influence them by ethical behavior.

Other than savoring the scraps of enjoyment randomly scattered throughout life, what can or should the wise person do before death erases his existence? Qohelet never uses the conventional wisdom phrase "fear [*yir'ât*] of God,"[16] but he urges "fear" (*yār'*) when standing before the deity, counsel that blurs the line between piety expressed as reverence and awe and piety expressed as terrorized submission (3:14; 5:7 [Heb. 5:6]; 7:18; 8:12). As far as Qohelet can see, God *effects* the collapse of wisdom's search for understanding, and with it all human endeavors to discern or construct a meaningful moral vision for life, *in order* to evoke trembling resignation to inscrutable sovereignty.[17] Whatever God does, God does "so that people are reverent before him" (*šeyyir'û millpānāyw*, 3:14).

Qohelet's Intellectual World

In what world of thought would Qohelet's perspectives on God and human existence have had an audience? A date in the mid-third century BCE places the author of Ecclesiastes in a cultural milieu shaped by the policies of the Ptolemaic rulers who succeeded Alexander the Great, particularly Ptolemy II Philadelphus (282–246 BCE) and his son, Ptolemy III Euergetes (246–221 BCE). The bureaucracy they constructed spread Hellenistic values and traditions throughout the empire, including Judah, which, until Alexander the Great's defeat of Darius, had been under Persian control for more than two hundred years (539–333 BCE). Royal land grants promoted the dispersion of Greek citizens into colonized territories and secured their loyalty through the collection of a yearly rent, which made clear the land belonged to the crown and could be reclaimed at any time. Conquered natives, like the Jews in Jerusalem, had measured freedom to manage their economic and religious affairs, so long as they peacefully complied with imperial policies, including a taxation system that could be capriciously revised at any time.

Commerce was fueled by a monetary system of minted coins. Ptolemy II increased coinage more than four times what it had been during the rule of his father,[18] an indicator that in Judah as throughout the empire a strong economy created wealth for those who could take advantage of the opportunities. The Zenon papyri preserve the reports of a Ptolemaic business manager who visited Jerusalem circa 259 BCE. These documents confirm the wealth of well-connected Jews of this period. Tobias, for example, the brother-in-law of the high priest Onias II, writes two letters to Apollonos, a financial advisor to Ptolemy II.

> Toubias to Apollonios greeting. If you and your affairs are flourishing, and everything else is as you wish it, many thanks to the gods! I too have been well, and thought of you at all times, as was right. I have sent to you Aineias bringing a eunuch and four boys, house-slaves of good stock, two of whom are uncircumcised. I append descriptions of the boys for your information.

> Toubias to Apollonios greeting. On the tenth of Xandikos I sent Aineias our servant, bringing gifts for the king which you wrote and asked me to send in the month of Xandikos: two horses, six dogs, one wild mule out of an ass, two white Arab donkeys, two wild mules' foals, one wild ass's foal. They are all tame. I have also sent you the letter which I have written to the king about the gifts, together with a copy for your information.[19]

In ancient societies as in modern ones, economic opportunity typically brings with it economic risks. Land given as a grant by the empire can be taken away without notice; the landed become landless. Taxes levied on goods and services can be raised without notice or cause; those who can pay what is required might weather the increase, but those who cannot fall precariously deeper into debt. Wealth is seductive; those who have it want to increase it and will take on greater and greater risks to do so. Poverty can likewise be all consuming. The poor become poorer, not by choice but because they have no choice; nothing they can do makes a difference.

Qohelet's first question, "What do people profit [*yitrôn*; CEB: 'gain'] from all the hard work?" (1:3, author's translation), likely reflects the unpredictability of the economy in Ptolemaic Judah. The word *yitrôn* is only found in Ecclesiastes, where it occurs ten times to describe either a return on a business investment (1:3; 2:11; 3:9; 5:9, 16 [Heb. 5:8, 15]; 7:11) or an advantage gained by choosing one thing over another (2:13 [two times]; 10:10, 11). Even if one had the unrestrained power of kings to acquire anything he wants, all his possessions together would add up to zero.

> I took on great projects: I built houses for myself, planted vineyards for myself. I made gardens and parks for myself, planting every kind of

fruit tree in them. I made reservoirs for myself to water my lush groves. I acquired male servants and female servants; I even had slaves born in my house. I also had great herds of cattle and sheep, more than any who preceded me in Jerusalem. I amassed silver and gold for myself, the treasures of kings and provinces. I acquired male and female singers for myself, along with every human luxury, treasure chests galore! . . . But when I surveyed all that my hands had done, and what I had worked so hard to achieve, I realized that it was pointless—a chasing after wind. Nothing is to be gained [*yitrôn*] under the sun. (2:4-8, 11)

It is unclear whether Qohelet refers to the acquisitions of Ptolemaic rulers ("kings" and "provinces") or of the Jerusalem elite—the priests, the wealthy (e.g., Tobias), and the learned (e.g., Qohelet, the "Teacher" who imagines himself a king)—but it is certain that "the money lover isn't satisfied with money; neither is the lover of wealth satisfied with income" (5:10; Heb. 5:9). From Qohelet's perspective, it does not matter who pulls the economic levers, because God gives the wealth and riches people hoard as their own, and God randomly takes it away and gives it to others (6:1-2). In the mercantile world of Ptolemaic Judah, everything is a commodity, something to be assessed according to the metrics of profit and loss, benefit and value, even knowledge, wisdom, and enjoyment (2:26; 6:9; 7:11-12; 9:16, 18; 10:10).

Ptolemaic financial policies may provide the immediate background for Qohelet's observations on the pointlessness of materialism, but the spread of Hellenistic culture throughout Judah in the third century BCE was also inextricably intertwined with an intellectual economy that traced its origins to Aristotle and his stewardship of Socratic philosophy. Aristotle, who tutored Alexander the Great, died in 333 BCE. In the wake of his death, the Socratic tradition that he and his teacher Plato had debated diffused into four primary schools of thought, each identified with a founding figure: Cynicism (Diogenes, ca. 412–323 BCE); Stoicism (Zeno, 344–262 BCE); Skepticism (Pyrrho, 360–270 BCE); and Epicureanism (Epicurus, 341–270 BCE). Each of these schools found in the Socratic dialogues a model for reflecting on a common question, "How should one live?" Plato reported that Socrates himself answered the question by affirming a contradiction: "I do not think I know what I do not know" (*Apology*, 21d).[20]

The Hellenistic philosophers who followed Socrates posed their own versions of the same question. In good Socratic fashion they interacted with each other by analyzing the strengths and weaknesses of a variety of possible answers, then offered their own nuanced conclusions. The Cynics argued that the highest goal in life is virtue, which is not only its own reward but also the only reward worth having. Toward that end, they typically withdrew from society, shunned social convention, and adopted a life of poverty and self-sufficiency. The Stoics also argued that the goal of the philosophical life is wisdom and virtue; although they did not withdraw from society as the Cynics did, they did advocate what we would call a "stoic indifference" (*apatheia*, "without passion") to its regnant values. Skeptics focused on Socrates's constant questioning. How can we be sure that we know what we think we know? Whereas Socrates claimed that he himself did not know the full truth about anything, the Skeptic (*skeptikos*, "inquirer, questioner, learner") extended his observation by insisting that no one could be certain about anything, including the true path to wisdom, knowledge, and virtue. The truly wise person suspends judgment and continues the inquiry, yielding neither to unfounded belief (*doxa*) nor to unquestioned knowledge. Skepticism, this school argued, was not a concession to disabling doubt; it was instead a generative way of searching for truth. Epicureans saw pleasure as the greatest good in life and wisdom as paramount for measuring what will produce the most pleasure and the least pain. Socrates provides the starting point for the Epicureans' philosophy of hedonism in his dialogue with Protagoras:

> Weighing is a good analogy; you put the pleasures together and the pains together, both the near and the remote, on the balance scale, and then say which of the two is more. For if you weigh pleasant things against pleasant things, the greater and the more must always be taken; if painful things against painful, the fewer and the smaller. And if you weigh pleasant things against painful, and the painful is exceeded by the pleasant—whether the near by the remote or the remote by the near— you have to perform that action in which the pleasant prevails; on the

other hand, if the pleasant is exceeded by the painful, you have to refrain from doing that. (*Protagoras*, 356b-c)

There is no clear evidence that Qohelet borrowed directly from Hellenistic philosophy, but there can be little doubt that he participated in the intellectual discourse it generated, often replicating its method of inquiry in order to reach his own conclusions.[21] A few examples must suffice.

(1) Socratic inquiry typically uses questions to invite consideration of multiple ways of thinking about an issue, as in Socrates's exploration of the question "What is knowledge?" with Theaetetus:

Socrates: Now isn't it true that to learn is to become wiser about the thing one is learning?

Theaetetus: Yes, of course.

Socrates: And what makes men wise, I take it, is wisdom?

Theaetetus: Yes.

Socrates: And is this in any way different from knowledge?

Theaetetus: What?

Socrates: Wisdom. Isn't it the things which they know that men are wise about?

Theaetetus: Well, yes.

Socrates: So knowledge and wisdom will be the same thing?

Theaetetus: Yes.

Socrates: Now this is just where my difficulty comes in. (*Theaetetus*, 145d-e)

After a lengthy back-and-forth discussion about the difficulties in grasping the essence of knowledge, Socrates concludes by saying:

And so, Theaetetus, if ever in the future you should attempt to conceive or should succeed in conceiving other theories, they will be better ones as the result of this inquiry. And if you remain barren, your companions will find you gentler and less tiresome; you will be modest and not think you know what you don't know. This is all my art can achieve—nothing more. (*Theaetetus*, 210c)

The opening words of the Qohelet's first poem introduce a similar Socratic mode of questioning, "What do people gain from all the hard work that they work so hard at under the sun?" (1:3; cf. 2:11; 3:9; 5:16 [Heb. 5:15]; 6:8, 11). Other questions throughout the book introduce a variety of observations, for example:

> Why have I been so very wise? (2:15)
>
> Who knows whether that one will be wise or foolish? (2:19)
>
> Who knows if a human being's life-breath rises upward while an animal's life-breath descends into the earth? (3:21)
>
> Who, really, is able to see what will happen in the future? (3:22)
>
> Isn't everyone heading to the same destination? (6:6)
>
> Who can straighten what God has made crooked? (7:13)
>
> Who can grasp [what happens in life]? (7:24)
>
> Who is wise? And who knows the meaning of anything? (8:1)

There is however a different rationale behind Qohelet's questioning. Socratic inquiry typically opens up the thinking process by suspending final judgment as long as there are more questions to ask. The objective is to expand the intellectual search by remaining open to new discoveries, not to restrict it or eliminate it by claiming to have obtained ultimate answers. Socrates expects Theaetetus to continue his quest for knowledge, not to abandon it. Qohelet's questions, by contrast, are merely rhetorical. Qohelet has already determined the final answers. What profit is there in labor? None. Is there not one and the same fate for everyone? Yes. Who knows the meaning of anything? No one. The answers resolve the questions. The Teacher's (1:1-2) certainty ironically ends the student's quest for new knowledge. There is nothing more to discover and so therefore no reason to continue the learning process. "Whatever has happened— that's what will happen again," Qohelet announces without equivocation, "whatever has occurred—that's what will occur again. There's nothing new under the sun" (1:9; cf. 3:15; 6:10).

(2) Among the oldest examples of Cynic writing is the diatribe (*diatribe*, literally, "a rubbing or wearing away"), a learned discourse that takes a position against a person or a belief, essentially an argument that seeks to "erase" an idea. Compositions by Teles, a Greek teacher from Megara writing in the middle of the third century BCE, thus perhaps Qohelet's contemporary, provide insight into the form and structure of a diatribe. A teacher first introduces a thesis, then develops a dialogue that refutes it. Sometimes the one the teacher addresses speaks, thus producing a Socratic interchange between teacher and student; at other times the teacher engages in a "dialogue" with himself (e.g., *dokei moi*, "it seems to me"), in effect talking to himself and listening for the strengths and weaknesses in what he is thinking.[22] Excerpts from Teles's writings on wealth and poverty provide examples.

(Thesis) It seems to me [*dokei moi*] that the acquisition of money frees one from scarcity and want.

(Question introducing refutation) And just how [*kai pōs*]? Don't you see that some men have acquired large sums, as they think, but do not use them because of illiberality and meanness? (IVA, lines 1-5)

(Thesis) Poverty is a deterrent to being a philosopher, but wealth is a useful thing for this.

(Refutation and development) Not well spoken. For how many men do you think have been kept from inactivity because of wealth rather than because of want? Or don't you see that, in general, the poorest men are philosophers, but the wealthy are involved in every activity because of these very possessions? . . . For how could you demonstrate that men are kept from being philosophers because of want as they are because of wealth? Or don't you see that because of poverty they are compelled to endure patiently, but because of wealth there is the reverse situation? For in my opinion, whenever a man happens to be easily provided with whatever he desires, he is no longer interested in working or making any philosophical investigation, but with wealth as co-worker in his wickedness, he refrains from no pleasure. . . .

Or again, don't ordinary household slaves support themselves and pay a fee to their master, while the free man will be unable to support himself? Therefore, it seems to me [*moi dokei*] that the unemployed man, freed from such cares, enjoys his inactivity more because he has nothing. (IVB, lines 1-5, 13-23, 34-39)[23]

Qohelet does not use the Greek diatribe form as such, but he does repeatedly talk to himself. Like Teles, he carries on an internal debate about what he sees, thinks, and believes. The use of two key words throughout the book is instructive, the first-person pronoun "I" and the word "heart." The pronoun "I" (*'ănî*) occurs twenty-nine times in Ecclesiastes, one indicator that the book has significant interest in Qohelet's self-searching and self-understanding, thus the frequency of the expressions "I see," and "I know."[24] The word "heart" (*lēb*) occurs forty-two times in the book, a higher statistical frequency than other key words like *hebel* ("pointless") and *'ĕlōhîm* ("God"). Of particular significance are the occasions when Qohelet talks to or with his heart about the search for knowledge and wisdom, for example:

> I said to myself [*dibbartî 'anî 'im libbî*, literally, "I spoke with my heart"], Look here, I have grown much wiser than any who ruled over Jerusalem before me. My mind has absorbed [*wĕlibbî rā'â*, literally, "my heart saw"] great wisdom and knowledge. But when I set my mind [*wā'ettnâ libbî*, literally, "gave my heart"] to understand wisdom, and also to understand madness and folly, I realized that this too was just wind chasing. (1:16-17; cf. 1:13)

> I said to myself [*'āmartî 'anî bĕlibbî*; literally, "I spoke with my heart"], Come, I will make you experience pleasure; enjoy what is good! . . . I tried cheering myself with wine and by embracing folly—with wisdom still guiding me—until I might see what is really worth doing in the few days that human beings have under heaven. (2:1, 3)

> I thought to myself [*'āmartî 'ănî bĕlibbî*; literally, "I spoke with my heart"], God will judge both righteous and wicked people. . . . I also thought [*'āmartî 'ănî bĕlibbî*, literally, "I spoke with my heart"], Where human beings are concerned, God tests them to show them that they are but animals. (3:17-18)[25]

When Qohelet speaks with his heart, he finds himself locked into an internal debate, essentially a diatribe against himself, where contradictory facts erase each other and stalemate the search for understanding. Every "yes" statement is qualified by a following "but":[26]

Pleasure is "madness" and of no use at all (2:10-11, 23), but "there's nothing better for human beings than to eat, drink, and experience pleasure in their hard work" (2:24-26; cf. 5:18-20 [Heb. 5:17-19]; 8:15).

Wealth is good (5:9 [Heb. 5:8]; 6:8; 7:11), but it has no lasting value (5:10-14 [Heb. 5:9-13]).

Qohelet "hates" life (2:17) but affirms that life is better than death (9:4-6; 11:7).

God judges the righteous and the wicked (3:17; 5:6 [Heb. 5:4]; 8:12-13; 11:9), but "the righteous get what the wicked deserve, and the wicked get what the righteous deserve" (8:14; cf. 8:10; 9:2-3).

Wisdom is better than foolishness (2:13; 7:11, 19; 9:16-18; 10:2-3), but what happens to the fool also happens to the wise (1:17-18; 2:15-16; 6:8; 10:1).

If a teacher's diatribe is meant to convince students that they should believe one thing and not another, then Qohelet's divided heart/mind leaves his students adrift in a sea of indistinguishable options. There is neither a rational (mind) nor a non-rational (heart) motivation for making a decision. To paraphrase Socrates's words to Theaetetus, "There is indecision; this is the only 'choice' one has—nothing more."

(3) Qohelet's repeated commendation of pleasure—"eat, drink, and enjoy" (3:13)—resonates with Epicurean philosophy, but it shares neither its rationale nor its objective. One instinctively seeks pleasure (*hēdonē*), Epicurus argued, because it is causally connected with the good. The pleasure of eating is good because it reduces hunger; the pleasure of drinking is good because it quenches thirst. The objective of seeking pleasure is in all cases the same: the elimination of discomfort, disturbance, or pain. Viewed in this way, hedonic pleasure becomes the sole criterion for

83

navigating life's choices; one seeks X instead of Y because there is a predictable good outcome that comes with X, and an equally predictable negative outcome with Y. As Epicurus puts it, "[W]e call pleasure the alpha and omega of a blessed life. Pleasure is our first and kindred good. It is the starting point of every choice and of every aversion, and to it we come back, . . . to judge of every good thing."[27]

In sum, for Epicurus, pleasure enlarges and enhances life by reducing its variables. The benefit of "sober reasoning" [*nēphon logismos*] and wisdom [or *phronēsis*, "prudence"] is to know that pleasure is the highest good; it and it alone makes life meaningful and satisfying.

> [I]t is sober reasoning [*nēphon logismos*], searching out the grounds of every choice and avoidance, and banishing those beliefs . . . . Of all this the beginning and the greatest good is prudence [*phronēsis*]. Wherefore prudence [*phronēsis*] is a more precious thing even than philosophy; from it spring all other virtues.[28]

Qohelet sees no connection between pleasure and good, no reason to believe that eating, drinking, and enjoyment is a good that has any lasting value. Hunger and thirst may be assuaged, but any pleasure one derives from eating and drinking lasts only until the next craving. Pleasure cannot be attained by choice; it is an unpredictable sensation that is indifferent to a person's needs or wants. God doles out pleasure to one and pain to another, but there is no rational explanation for God's decisions (2:24-26). Human wisdom cannot make the incomprehensible comprehensible.

Moreover, as far as Qohelet can see, pleasure is not a benefit that enhances life by increasing the good; it is instead the residue of life, what is left over after God has subtracted everything else of value. It represents an "ensmallment" of life, not an enlargement; it requires accommodation, not resistance. The only certainty Qohelet can discern when he puts pleasure to the test (2:1-11) is that it is essentially a synonym for pointlessness. Embedded within the seven *carpe diem* statements is the reminder that hedonic pleasure is not the antidote for *hebel*;[29] it is both the cause and the consequence.

> God gives wisdom, knowledge, and joy to those who please God. . . .
> This too is pointless [*hebel*] and a chasing after wind. (2:26)

Sweet is the light, and it's pleasant for the eyes to see the sun. Even those
who live many years should take pleasure in them all. But they should be
mindful that there will also be many dark days. Everything that happens
is pointless [*hebel*]. (11:7; cf. vv. 9-10)

In an upside-down world where *hebel*, not joy, is the criterion for measuring the meaning of life, Qohelet teaches his students to enjoy "all the days
of your pointless life [*kāl yĕmê ḥayyē heblekā*]—because that's your part to
play in this life" (9:9). Pleasure is pointless and pointlessness is pleasure.

Qohelet and Epicurus were both hedonists when viewed through the
lens of Hellenistic philosophy, but they assessed the benefits of this perspective on life in very different ways. Epicurus is a satisfied hedonist;
he trusts that pleasure attained promises the beginning and ending of a
blessed life. Qohelet is a resigned hedonist; he concedes that random experiences of fleeting pleasures are all that a meaningless life has to offer.

In the ways noted above, the author of Ecclesiastes shows that he is
familiar with the underlying skepticism that characterized much of Hellenistic philosophy. The search for wisdom, however, did not begin in the
fifth century BCE with Socrates and the Athenians. It has its roots in an
international Wisdom tradition that begins two thousand years earlier in
Egypt and Mesopotamia, then spreads to Syria and Palestine. It is productive not only in the contiguous ancient Near Eastern cultures that influenced Israelite wisdom but also in intellectual discourse dating at least to
the second millennium BCE in India, China, and the Far East.[30] The wide
orbit of ancient wisdom is a reminder that in the third century BCE the
author of Ecclesiastes was participating in a long slipstream of wisdom
thinking sustained by many diverse voices.

The heterodox views of Qohelet (and Job) may reflect an internal crisis within Israelite wisdom. Older wisdom texts like the book of Proverbs,
especially the maxims in chapters 10–29 that are generally dated to the
eighth to seventh centuries BCE, are typically positive in their assessment
of the moral order of the world and the divine justice that sustains it.
"Those who trust the LORD are secure" (Prov 29:25), according to wisdom's orthodoxy; whatever the limits of human understanding, intelligent people will "keep quiet" (Prov 11:12; cf. 10:19; 12:23; 13:3; 17:28).

Qohelet scrutinizes this view and declares it wholly inadequate. Chaos, injustice, and divine indifference to the utter meaninglessness of life expose conventional wisdom as a fraud; invincible realities "turn the wise into fools" (Eccl 7:7). Qohelet's skepticism is the "dead flies [that] spoil the perfumer's oil" (Eccl 10:1); he (and Job) represents the fracture in orthodoxy's claim to absolute truth.

However destabilizing Qohelet's skepticism might have been in the third century BCE, it was not an uncommon perspective in the ancient Near East, and its permeation of religious orthodoxy was not limited to Ptolemaic Judah. In the second millennium BCE Egyptian text, "The Complaints of Khakheperre-Sonb," a man meditates on the troubles in the land that the transmitted wisdom of the ancestors cannot explain.

> The land breaks up, is destroyed
>
> Becomes [a wasteland],
>
> Order is cast out,
>
> Chaos is in the council hall;
>
> The ways of the gods are violated,
>
> Their provisions are neglected. . . .
>
> None is wise enough to know it.

With despair that anticipates Qohelet's resignation, the man concedes that it is too painful to be silent, and it is "futile" to speak.[31]

A number of pessimistic wisdom texts from Mesopotamia are reminiscent of Qohelet. "The Babylonian Theodicy" is a first millennium BCE acrostic poem that records a dialogue between a sufferer who complains about injustice and a friend who defends orthodox perspectives.[32] The dialogue highlights the contradictions between the oracles' assurances (49) about the plan of the gods and what the one who "looked around society" discovered when he saw that "the evidence is contrary" (243). "The rogue has been promoted," the sufferer says, "but I have been brought low" (77).

"Counsels of a Pessimist" is a text from the Ashurbanipal library in Nineveh, Assyria, probably dated to the first millennium. Like Qohelet,

the speaker reflects on the transitory nature of human life and work—
"[Whatever] men do does not last for ever" (l. 109)—and like the orthodox voice that speaks in Proverbs and in the appendix to the book of
Ecclesiastes (12:9-14), the writer urges the reader to submit to the mystery
of the divine:

> [As for] you, offer prayers to (your) god . . .
>
> Bow down to your city goddess that she may grant you offspring.[33]

The Babylonian text "The Dialogue of Pessimism" is between a master
and his slave concerning what is the right and worthy thing to do among a
variety of options. The master asks if he should drive to the palace or enjoy
a satisfying meal or go home to his family or lead a revolution or perform
a public benefit. After weighing the pros and cons of all the possibilities,
the master arrives in despair at his final question, "What, then, is good?"
(cf. Eccl 6:12: "Who knows what's good for human beings during life,
during their brief pointless life?"). The slave answers that death would be
preferable to a life without discoverable purpose:

> To have my neck and your neck broken
>
> And to be thrown into the river is good."[34]

When Qohelet claims to have applied himself "to explore by wisdom
all that happens under heaven" (1:13), and when he concludes that "all
that happens is elusive and utterly unfathomable" (7:24), he is engaging
an international wisdom tradition that had long resisted closure. Qohelet's
epilogist will claim to have heard all that could be said about these matters and to have come to a final and convincing resolution: "Worship God
and keep God's commandments because this is what everyone must do"
(12:13). Located as it is within the wisdom tradition, however, this assertion, like all claims to absolute truth, merits investigation.

The End of the Matter

At the beginning of this chapter, I suggested readers might find the
key to the rhetorical strategy of this book in its repetition of key words and

themes. The last words in the book, which is the appendix in 12:13-14, invite readers to (re)consider certain ones of these key terms in light of the epilogist's assertion that we have now come to "the end of the matter" (*sôp dābār hakkōl nišmāʿ*, v. 13a).

The Teacher began by asserting that the whole (*kōl*) of human existence is "perfectly pointless" (*hăbel hăbālîm hakkōl hābel*, 1:2). The epilogist concludes by declaring that because "all has been heard" (*hakkōl nišmāʿ*), the book is now complete. The inference is that all that can or needs to be said about the matters discussed in this book has been said. The word "all" (*kōl*) occurs ninety-one times in Ecclesiastes; the epilogist uses this word four times in two verses, an indication that he aims at a similar comprehensiveness: "all has been heard"; "everyone" (*kol hāʾādām*, v. 13b, literally, "all of humankind"); "every deed" (*kol măʿăśeh*); "every hidden thing" (*kol neʿlām*). The phrase "perfectly pointless" (*hebel*), which occurs thirty-eight times throughout the book, is not included in the last two verses, but the word for "(the) God" (*hāʾĕlōhîm*), which occurs only slightly more frequently (forty times) than *hebel*, occurs twice in the final two verses and is implied a third time by the use of a pronoun ("his"). All three God-references are associated with imperatives for piety that occur here for the first time in the book: "Worship God [literally, 'fear the God'] and keep God's [Heb: 'his'] commandments."[35] If there is a rough equivalence between *hebel* and "God" throughout Qohelet's message, a statistical—perhaps ideological and/or theological—stalemate that leaves it unclear who or what has the upper hand in Qohelet's world, then that ambiguity is no longer present in the book's final verses.[36] When all is said and done, the epilogist concludes, everything human wisdom perceives as pointless ultimately gives way to divine purpose: "God will definitely bring every deed to judgment, including every hidden thing, whether good or bad" (*ʾim ṭôb wĕʾim rāʿ*, literally, "good and evil")."

In Socratic fashion, readers may probe the strengths and weaknesses of this final assertion. Is the whole of human existence pointless, as Qohelet consistently argues (e.g., 1:2 and 12:7)? Or is its purpose, hidden though it may often seem, secure in the hands of a just and righteous God? Underlying both questions is another and still more fundamental one: how can one know? Given the intellectual ethos of this book, the question is likely as important as the answer. Qohelet and the epilogist offer two contrasting perspectives that are central for understanding how the wisdom tradition addressed these matters.

Qohelet relies on personal observation. He does not typically draw upon the proverbial wisdom of the ancestors (e.g., Prov 10–29);[37] he does not turn to truth as revealed by God (e.g., the prophets). He adopts instead a fundamental tenet of the intellectual inquiry that characterizes the Greek philosophy of his day, the autonomy of human reason.[38] He learns by observing with his own eyes, by thinking his own thoughts, by finding and acquiring knowledge on his own. The investigation process is open-ended until and unless some truth emerges that satisfactorily subordinates curiosity. Qohelet's search for wisdom seems to be unsuccessful, since he concludes that he cannot find the answers he is looking for (e.g., 1:16-17; 7:23-25; 8:16-17). Even so, he arrives at this conclusion on his own; he does not simply accept it as truth received from some external source that cannot be examined.

The epilogist uses some (not all) of Qohelet's vocabulary, as noted above, but his words convey assertions not questions, imperatives that command decisions not observations that invite consideration of multiple options. The brevity of his words may be nothing other than the result of an ancient transmission process that has not preserved a longer version; alternatively, his words may convey a conviction that neither requires nor invites further comment. In either case, the epilogist has the final word in the canonical version of this book. It is a word that brings matters to an end by adding things to what Qohelet has said that were lacking before— the requisites of fear of God and obedience to Torah—and subtracting things that likely seemed to the epilogist unnecessary, unwise, or inappropriate, especially the conclusion that all is *hebel.*

What if? What if Qohelet's epilogist does in fact have the final and most convincing argument? The removal of doubt and the gain of certainty surely provide welcome relief for incessant questioning that seems to lead nowhere and accomplish nothing. When an authoritative decision eliminates unwise choices, leaving only one sure path ahead, the way forward becomes more direct, the destination clearer. In principle, Qohelet would not disagree. He recognizes "the advantage of knowledge" (7:12) but concedes that the search for wisdom can be "an unhappy obsession" (1:13) that results in more aggravation and less serenity (1:18). It is better to be content with what is given than to grind away at what is beyond reach (4:6). The epilogist speaks with authority that approximates that of personified Wisdom in Proverbs. As one intimate with the God of all wisdom, the epilogist speaks what is "correct," "right," and "true"; he has found the "knowledge" Qohelet seeks (see Prov 8:4-12). The sum and substance of the epilogist's truth—"the end of the matter"—is this: the imperative for obedience to God subordinates human knowledge to divine wisdom. One commentator exegetes this imperative as follows:

> By giving piety the final word, the postscript blunts the thorns imminent in the roamings of the human intellect at the very same time it allows Qoheleth—and other intellectuals—freedom of movement for their inquiries. All wisdom may be heard and considered, so long as it is finally subject to the controls of piety in attitude and behavior. Qoheleth pushes wisdom to the edge. The last verse marks the boundary. To use God's words to Job (38:11): "This far you may come, but no farther."[39]

Does the imperative for obedience to divinely revealed truth subordinate intellectual curiosity to piety? What if Qohelet has the better argument? What if his observation about the incomprehensibility of life—in relation to others and to God—is consistent with the reality humans see and experience? What would be gained by embracing this truth? What would be lost by ignoring or denying it? From Qohelet's perspective, the key to assessing gains and losses is the value placed on the human capacity for new discoveries, for knowledge acquired by reasoning independent of (not hostile to) external authority. Every intellectual quest necessarily reckons with the possibility that reasonable questions may exceed the grasp of any rational explanation. The underlying premise of Qohelet's argument, however, is that the quest is valuable in and of itself because questions about ultimate matters make possible penultimate discoveries.

Qohelet's ultimate curiosity is his wonderment about the sense of the whole (3:11; CEB: "eternity") that God has placed within the human heart, the elusive portion of the infinite that can make the whole comprehensible for finite mortals, if they could but discover it. Qohelet does not attain this ultimate knowledge; nonetheless, his search for the infinite within the finite, the divine that is both within and beyond the human, represents a penultimate discovery of no small consequence.[40] To be created in the image of God, as Qohelet understands it, is to stand on the other side of Eden as flawed but divinely gifted human beings and to say "yes" to the invitation to build a life that is "very good." One commentator exegetes what is at stake when one considers the merits of Qohelet's message as follows:

> The effect of cutting off debate is to render opponents silent. The victory, however, is Pyrrhic. That is the force of the summation in verse 13a: "End of the matter; everything has been heard." What a bold claim. Precious little in Qoheleth's teaching reads like a closed book. Matters are left tentative, issues unresolved, as if challenging hearers and readers to carry the argument further. True, Qoheleth made absolutist claims about everything being *hebel*, but he often examined competing perceptions without tipping his hand about his preference. For him there was no end, for each answer opened up to another question, or two.[41]

However readers may weigh the message of Qohelet against the words of his epilogist, the book of Ecclesiastes does represent an end of sorts, or at least a significant transition in Jewish wisdom literature. The books of Proverbs, Job, and Ecclesiastes were canonized in both the Hebrew Bible and the Protestant Old Testament. Sirach and the Wisdom of Solomon are included among the apocryphal or deuterocanonical works that fall within the intertestamental period. Their contributions to Jewish wisdom will be discussed in the following chapters. At this juncture, however, we may pause to offer an observation concerning the canonical books we have overviewed thus far.

The final forms of Proverbs, Job, and Ecclesiastes suggest that a persistent tension between piety and intellect lay at the center of ancient Israel's wisdom tradition. Proverbs frames older folk, largely secular wisdom sayings with an introduction (chapters 1–9) and a conclusion (chapter 31) that set these sayings within a more explicitly theological context. The final form thus combines an intellectualization of piety with a piety of intellectualism.[42] The book of Job frames a lengthy and unresolved debate between Job and his friends about divine injustice (Job 3:1–42:6) with a prologue and epilogue (Job 1–2, 42:7-14) that resolve the debate by contextualizing it within an assertion about God's providence. In different ways, both Proverbs and Job make the case for a fundamental truth that overrides all debate: the fear of the Lord is the beginning of wisdom (e.g., Prov 1:7; Job 28:28). Qohelet's epilogist exemplifies a similar approach; once again, uncertainties disclosed through the human pursuit of knowledge are subordinated to inscrutable divine wisdom.

If the epilogist's objective was to bring an end once and for all to the search for knowledge and wisdom in Judah or in the Hellenistic world of his time, he did not succeed. In the Jewish tradition, the authors of Sirach and Wisdom continued the quest, although as we shall see their orthodoxy carefully circumscribed open-ended questions. In the Greco-Roman world, which was the historical setting for Sirach and Wisdom of Solomon, Socratic philosophy constituted the center of an intellectual economy that endured for at least a thousand years.

For Further Reading

Barbour, J. *The Story of Israel in the Book of Qohelet: Ecclesiastes as Cultural Memory.* Oxford: Oxford University Press, 2012.

Boda, M. J., T. Longmann III, and C. G. Rata, eds. *The Words of the Wise Are Like Goads: Engaging Qohelet in the 21st Century.* Winona Lake, IN: Eisenbrauns, 2013.

Bundvad, M. *Time in the Book of Ecclesiastes.* Oxford: Oxford University Press, 2015.

Crenshaw, J. L. *Qohelet: The Ironic Wink.* Studies on Personalities of the Old Testament. Columbia: University of South Carolina Press, 2013.

Dell, K. J. *Interpreting Ecclesiastes: Readers Old and New*. Winona Lake, IN: Eisenbrauns, 2013.

Douglas, J. N. *A Polemical Preacher of Joy: An Anti-apocalyptic Genre for Qoheleth's Message of Joy*. Eugene, OR: Pickwick, 2008.

Fox, M. V. *Qoheleth and His Contradictions*. JSOTSup 71. Sheffield, UK: Almond Press, 1989.

Ingram, D. *Ambiguity in Ecclesiastes*. LHBOTS 431. London: T & T Clark, 2006.

Koh, Y. V. *Royal Autobiography in the Book of Qoheleth*. BZAW 369. Berlin: Walter de Gruyter, 2006.

Lee, E. P. *The Vitality of Enjoyment in Qohelet's Theological Rhetoric*. BZAW 353. Berlin: Walter de Gruyter, 2005.

Limburg, J. *Encountering Ecclesiastes: A Book for Our Time*. Grand Rapids, MI: William B. Eerdmans, 2006.

Miller, D. B. *Symbol and Rhetoric in Ecclesiastes: The Place of Hebel in Qohelet's Work*. Atlanta: Society of Biblical Literature, 2002.

Ogden, G. S. *Qoheleth*. Sheffield, UK: Sheffield Academic Press, 2007.

Salyer, G. *Vain Rhetoric: Private Insight and Public Debate in Ecclesiastes*. Sheffield, UK: Sheffield Academic Press, 2001.

Schoors, A., ed. *Qohelet in the Context of Wisdom*. Leuven: Leuven University Press, 1988.

Shields, M. *The End of Wisdom: A Reappraisal of the Historical and Canonical Function of Ecclesiastes*. Winona Lake, IN: Eisenbrauns, 2006.

Sneed, M. R. *The Politics of Pessimism in Ecclesiastes: A New Social Science Approach*. Atlanta: Society of Biblical Literature, 2012.

Stone, T. J. *The Compilational History of the Megilloth: Canon, Contoured Intertextuality and Meaning in the Writings*. Tübingen: Mohr Siebeck, 2013.

Chapter 4
Sirach

"All Wisdom Involves Doing the Law"

For the first time in Israel's wisdom literature, a prologue introduces readers to the author, date, setting, and objective of a sapiential text. In three stylishly crafted Greek sentences (numbered in English: 1-14, 15-26, 27-34), the grandson of Jesus ben Sirach (cf. 50:27: "Jesus, Sirach's son") reports that he has translated a Hebrew work dealing with "education [*paideia*] and wisdom [*sophia*]" (12) composed by his grandfather, who had devoted himself to studying "the Law, the Prophets, and the other ancestral scrolls" (8-10; cf. 24-25).[1] The grandson found a copy of this book when he arrived in Egypt "in the thirty-eighth year of the rule of King Euergetes" (27). The reference is to Eugeretes II Ptolemy VII Physkon, who ruled Egypt 170–164 and 146–117 BCE. The thirty-eighth year of this reign is 132 BCE. The book the grandson discovered contains a lengthy eulogy for the Jewish High Priest Simon II (50:1-24), who died in 196 BCE, but makes no mention of the Seleucid ruler Antiochus IV Epiphanes (175–164 BCE) and the Syrian oppression that triggered the Maccabean revolt in 167 BCE. Ben Sira's work was therefore likely composed between 195 and 175 BCE and translated, after his grandson "worked skillfully and stayed up many nights to bring the scroll to completion" (31-32), between 132 and 117 BCE. The setting for the translation is probably Alexandria; the addressees are Jews living outside Palestine "who want to become well educated" (34, *philomathein*, literally, "to love

95

learning and study"). The primary objective of the book, the grandson declares, is to teach all "lovers of learning" (13, *philomatheis*) to live "according to the Law" (14, 34, *ennomou bioseōs*).

The prologue's correlation of wisdom (*sophia*, 3, 12) and law (*nomos*, 14, 34) introduces a new synthesis that responds to the discourse and debate in Proverbs, Job, and Ecclesiastes. Proverbs affirms that "Wisdom begins with the fear of the LORD" (Prov 1:7; cf. 9:10). The same affirmation occurs at the end of the debate between Job and his three friends. "Wisdom, where can it be found?" The sage who has examined the search process responds, "Look, the fear of the LORD is wisdom" (Job 28:28). The appendix to Ecclesiastes attempts to move the discourse, now pushed to the limits of orthodoxy, to the same conclusion: "This is the end of the matter. . . . Worship God and keep God's commandments" (Eccl 12:13). Qohelet's epilogist speaks as if he had been one of Ben Sira's students: "Fearing the Lord is the whole of wisdom, and all wisdom involves doing the Law" (Sir 19:20; cf. 1:16; 21:11; 23:27).

Ben Sira's synthesis—fear of God, wisdom, and Law—marks a transition within Israel's wisdom tradition that is manifest in multiple ways. Proverbs, Job, and Ecclesiastes are included in the Hebrew Bible and are accorded canonical status in the Protestant Old Testament; Sirach and Wisdom of Solomon are not in the Hebrew Bible but are included in the Septuagint, the Greek translation of the Old Testament that Protestants regard as apocryphal and Roman Catholics as deuterocanonical. Proverbs, Job, and Ecclesiastes are written in Hebrew and date to the late Second Temple Period, before and just after Hellenism began to spread in relatively benign ways throughout Syria and Palestine; extant copies of Sirach and Wisdom are written in Greek and date to a later period (second century BCE to first century CE), when the tensions between the colonizers and the colonized were more intense and the choices for Jews between compliance and resistance were more consequential.[2]

The transition is not only formal but also substantive. With Sirach and Wisdom, Israel's sages definitively subordinate human wisdom to divine revelation. They assign the voices of protest and skepticism represented by Job and Qohelet to a tradition remembered but no longer commended. They find the more authoritative model for those who seek wisdom in Proverbs, where piety regulates intellectual inquiry and obedience to God's commandments is more important than autonomous knowledge.

Form, Structure, and Rhetorical Strategy

Ben Sira utilizes a variety of literary forms, in keeping with his extensive reading of the Law, the Prophets, and the other writings. *Hymns of praise* (1:1-10; 18:1-4; 39:12-35; 42:15–43:33; 50:22-24; 51:1-12) and *prayers of petition* (23:1-6; 36:1-22) model the two primary ways of calling on God in the Psalms. *Autobiographical or confessional statements* provide glimpses into Ben Sira's personal experience as a learner and teacher of wisdom (24:30-34; 33:16-18; 51:13-22). *Onomastica* (lists) enumerate gifts from God that evoke wonder and praise, for example, the four basic necessities of life in 29:21 (water, bread, clothing, and shelter) and the eight items that add comfort and satisfaction in 39:26 (fire for cooking and warmth, iron for making tools and weapons, salt, fine flour, milk, honey, wine, and oil for savory food) or the eight natural calamities that convey God's judgment of sinners in 39:28-31 (wind, fire, hail, famine, death, wild beasts, scorpions, and vipers). *Didactic narratives* convey instruction based on rational observation (16:24–17:14; 39:1-11).

By far the predominant literary form in Sirach is the *māšāl*, the proverb or maxim that is characteristic in the book of Proverbs. The basic form comprises two parallel lines and is most clearly illustrated in the 375 sayings in Proverbs 10:1–22:16. Ben Sira employs this form regularly to compare, contrast, and evaluate a variety of truths that evoke common consent, for example:

> Wisdom was created before everything else.
> Right understanding is as old as certainty. (1:4)

> Talkative people are feared in their city,
> and people who are reckless in speech will be hated. (9:18)

> Whoever digs a hole will fall into it,
> and whoever sets a trap will get caught in it. (27:26)

Hard work was created
for every person,

and a heavy yoke lies upon human beings. (40:1)

Two- or three-line stand-alone proverbs are not, however, Ben Sira's primary mode of teaching. He prefers instead to use a single proverb or a series of proverbs to introduce and then develop a wide range of both practical and theological topics. Examples can be found in almost every chapter of the book. The following suffice as an introduction.

On reverence for God and respect for priests:

Revere the Lord with your whole being,
and honor his priests.

With all your might love the one who made you,
and don't neglect his ministers.

Fear the Lord and honor the priest:
Give the priest his portion, just as you were commanded:
early produce, a sin offering, the gift of the shoulders,
the dedicatory offering, and the early produce from the holy things.
(7:29-31)

On friendship:

Whoever pricks an eye will make tears flow,
and whoever pricks a heart reveals its feelings.

Whoever throws a stone at birds scares them off,
and whoever insults a friend breaks up a friendship.

If you draw a sword on a friend, don't despair,
because there can be a way back.

If you speak harshly to a friend, don't be concerned,
because there can be reconciliation.

But in the case of reproach, arrogance, the revealing of a secret,
or a treacherous blow, any friend will flee.

Gain your neighbor's trust while they are poor,
so that when they are prosperous, you will be filled along with them.

In a time of distress remain with them.
>   so that when they inherit, you will be a joint heir.

Before there's a fire, a furnace has vapor and smoke;
>   so before bloodshed there are insults.

I won't be ashamed to shelter friends,
>   and I won't hide from them.

And if something bad happens to me because of them,
>   everyone who hears of it will be on guard against them. (22:19-26)

On grieving the dead:

My child, let your tears flow for the dead;
>   as one who is suffering terribly, give voice to your sorrow.

Lay out their bodies in accordance with their wishes,
>   and don't neglect their burial.

Let your crying be bitter and express your sorrow fervently,
>   and make your mourning worthy of them.

Mourn for one day or two so that there can be no criticism,
>   and then be comforted from your grief.

Too much grief can lead to death,
>   and grief in one's heart will sap one's strength.

Grief also lingers in misery,
>   and the life of the poor is a curse upon the heart.

Don't give your heart over to grief; stay away from it,
>   remembering your own end.

Don't forget that there's no coming back;
>   you won't do them any good, and you will hurt yourself.

Remember their sentence, because it's yours also:
>   "Yesterday it was I, and today it's you!"

When the dead are at rest, put their memory to rest,
>   and be comforted for them when their spirit has left. (38:16-23)

The literary forms Ben Sira employs are drawn primarily from the poetic books, especially earlier wisdom writings; but as the prologue notes, he was also thoroughly familiar with all of the scriptural literature available to him, including the Torah and the Prophets. His quotes, allusions, adaptations, and interpretations of older biblical texts prompt one commentator to describe him as "the prototype of the rabbis."[3] For example, from Genesis, he alludes to Adam (33:10; 40:1), Eve (25:24), Lot (16:8), Noah (17:12), and the flood (40:10); from the Sinai pericope (Exod 19 to Num 10), he appropriates references to the Canaanites, "a nation doomed to destruction" (16:9), the "six hundred thousand" Israelites who perished in the wilderness (16:10; cf. Exod 12:37), the "water made sweet" at Marah (38:5; cf. Exod 15:23-25), the covenant made with Moses (24:23), and the characterization of the God who restored a broken covenant as "compassionate and merciful" (2:11; cf. Exod 34:6-7).[4] From prophetic critique of the cult, he makes the case against the separation of ritual practice from ethical behavior (34:21-31; cf. Amos 5:21-25; Mic 6:6-8; Hos 6:4-16; Isa 1:10-17). In prophetic call narratives, he finds his model for Wisdom's presence before God in "the assembly of the Most High" (24:1-2; cf. Isa 6:1-13).

Ben Sira's immersion in the full scope of biblical history is particularly clear in "Hymn to the Ancestors" (44:1–50:24). He summons his students to be proud of the rich heritage that provides their identity in a Greek world: the distant ancestors, Enoch, Noah, Abraham, Isaac, and Jacob (44:15-23–49:14-16);[5] the exodus generation, Moses, Aaron, and Phinehas (44:23–46:10); leaders from the period of the judges and the united monarchy, Joshua and Caleb, Samuel, Nathan, David, and Solomon (46:11–47:22); kings and prophets of the northern kingdom, Rehoboam, Elijah, and Elisha (47:23–48:16); kings and prophets of the southern kingdom until the fall of Jerusalem, Hezekiah, Isaiah, Josiah, and Jeremiah (48:17–49:7); prophets and leaders during the periods of exile and restoration, Ezekiel, Zerubbabel, Joshua, and Nehemiah (49:8-13); and Simon, the High Priest who was Ben Sira's contemporary (50:1-24). In short, Ben Sira is the epitome of the ideal sage immersed in the study of scripture:

> Those who devote themselves
>> and think about the *Law of the Most High* are the exception.
> They will seek out the *wisdom of all the ancestors*,
>> and they will be occupied with *prophecies*.
> They will preserve the *stories of famous people*,
>> and they will penetrate the *subtle turns of parables*.

They will seek out the *hidden meanings of proverbs,*
    and will live with the *puzzles of parables.* ....
They will open their mouth in *prayer* and ask forgiveness for their sins. ....
Their *reasoning* and *knowledge* will remain on course,
    and they will ponder God's *mysteries.*
They will bring to light the *learning* of their *instruction,*
    and they will make the *laws of the Lord's covenant* their boast. (38:1-3,
        5b, 7-8; italics added).

In addition to his knowledge of biblical texts, Ben Sira claims to have learned from his travels outside Jerusalem (34:9-13). There are significant parallels between Sirach and the Greek poet Theogonis (sixth century BCE), whose work similarly focused on practical advice.

Sirach	**Theogonis**
There are friends who are companions at your table, but they won't stay during hard times. (6:10)	Many, for sure, are cup-and-trencher fans, but few a man's comrades in a grave matter. (115-16)
They will act as if your belongings are theirs, and they will be bold toward your household slaves. (6:11)	When I am in good plight my friends are many, if aught ill befall, there's but a few whose hearts are true. (697-698)
Talkative people are feared in their city, and people who are reckless in speech will be hated. (9:18)	To a talkative man silence is a sore burden, and his speech a weariness to his company; all hate him. (295-97)
A furnace tests the hardening of steel when it's dipped so wine tests the heart when the arrogant quarrel. (31:26)	Cunning men know gold and silver in the fire; and the mind of a man, e'en though he be very knowing, is shown by the wine which he taketh. (499-500) [6]

The parallels are not limited to Greek literature; there are also clear indications that Ben Sira was familiar with Egyptian wisdom literature. The description of the non-scribal occupations necessary for civilization in Sirach 38:24–39:11 is at least indirectly influenced by the second-millennium Egyptian instructional text, "The Satire on Trades." Ben Sira examines the occupations of the farmer, the master artisan, the smith, and the potter and concludes that none of these skilled workers is as valuable for the health and welfare of a society as the scribe (38:25-34), whose "reasoning and knowledge" brings to light the mysteries of God (39:1-11). In similar fashion, "The Satire on Trades" reviews some fifteen occupations, including the farmer, jewel-maker, smith, and potter and concludes there is nothing better than the work of the scribe: "It's the greatest of all callings; there's none like it in the land."[7] There are also strong similarities in both form and content between Sirach and "The Instruction of Papyrus Insinger," a Ptolemaic period Egyptian instruction text. Both texts use single-sentence maxims, both combine individual maxims into larger thematic collections, both place instructions on filial piety near the beginning of the overall collection and creation hymns near the end, both conclude thematic sections with a round of summary proverbs, and both treat a range of similar topics, for example, the education of children (Sir 30:1-13 and P. Insinger 8.21–9.20); behavior before powerful people (Sir 8:1-3 and P. Insinger 4.2-3); the vices and virtues of women (Sir 26:7-18 and P. Insinger 8.4-19); and the concern with honor and shame (Sir 13:9-13 and P. Insinger 10.12–11.23).[8] In sum, Ben Sira was immersed in the sapiential literature available in his world. Wherever he found wisdom and knowledge that he regarded as true, he did not hesitate to appropriate it for his own objectives.

There is no consensus on a unifying structure for Ben Sira's wide-ranging literary forms and thematic foci.[9] We can identify various stylistic features and the outline of an overall structure but not a clear and systematic organization of ideas. The fifty-one chapters divide into three parts (1:1–24:34; 25:1–43:33; and 44:1–50:24), framed by a prologue (1-35) and postscripts (50:25-29) and appendices (51:1-12, 13-30). In the first part, five poems on wisdom introduce the major sections (1:1-10;

1:11-30; 4:11-19; 6:18-37; 14:20–15:10), where conventional proverbs on practical matters predominate (e.g., parents, children, friends, wealth and poverty, and manners). Five poems punctuate the second part of the book as well (24:1-22; 29:1-20; 32:14-20; 39:12-35; 42:15–43:33), although their relation to individual sections is less clear than in the first half, an indication that the core of the book has grown by addition.[10] Practical instructions continue, but attention to theological and spiritual issues is more frequent (e.g., fear of God, good and evil, sin, sacrifice, prayer, and divine judgment). Part three, 44:1–50:24, "Praise to the Ancestors," is a lengthy panegyric of godly people from the primordial period to Ben Sira's day. Chapter 24, the poem on Wisdom and Law, stands at the midpoint of the book and creates a structural and thematic bridge that links the three major parts together.

Sirach: "Wisdom and Law"

I. The grandson's prologue (lines 1-35): "Numerous and wonderful things have been given to us through the Law"

II. Part I (1:1–24:34)

> 1:1–4:10
> Two introductory poems: 1:1-10, "All wisdom comes from the Lord" (1:1); 1:11-30: "Fearing the Lord is Wisdom's root." (1:20)

> 4:11–6:17
> Introductory poem: 4:11-19, "Wisdom will . . . take hold of those who seek her." (4:11)

> 6:18–14:19
> Introductory poem: 6:18-37, "My child, . . . welcome education, and you will continue to discover Wisdom." (6:18)

> 14:20–23:27
> Introductory poem: 14:20–15:10, "Happy are those who meditate on Wisdom and who reason intelligently." (14:20)

> 24:1–33:18
> Introductory poem: 24:1-22, "I [Wisdom] came forth from the mouth of the Most High." (24:3)

III. Part II (25:1–43:33)

> 25:1–33:18
> Poems: 29:1-20, "Those who show compassion will lend to a neighbor" (29:1); 32:14-20, "Whoever fears the Lord will accept instruction." (32:14)

> 33:19–38:23

> 38:24–41:13
> Poem: 39:12-35, "Raise your voice, give praise together, and bless the Lord for all his works." (39:14)

41:14–43:33
Poem: 42:15–43:33, "Now I'll call to mind the works of the Lord."
(42:15)

IV. Part III (44:1–50:24), "Praise to the Ancestors"

V. Postscripts (50:25-29)

    50:25-26
    50:27-29

VI. Appendices (51:1-30)

    51:1-12, "Prayer of Jesus, Sirach's son"
    51:13-30, Acrostic poem: "I sought Wisdom openly in my prayer."
    (51:13)

Ethos and Ethics

The ethos (Greek: *ēthos*) or environment of Ben Sira was Judah in the first quarter of the second century BCE. The turmoil created by the wars between the Seleucids and the Ptolemies was resolved, temporarily, by the victory of Antiochus III (223–187 BCE), who established Seleucid control over the Macedonian Empire, which extended to Judah. Simon, the High Priest in Jerusalem during Ben Sira's time, welcomed Antiochus into the city. Antiochus was generous in response to Jewish friendship, confident that nothing more than a soft Hellenizing of the Jews was necessary for political stability. When his successor Antiochus IV Epiphanes assumed the reins of power, a harder and more punitive form of Hellenism triggered a Jewish revolt, but for the duration of Antiochus's rule, there was a mutually beneficial relationship between the colonizer and the colonized, so long as the Jews remained loyal subjects of the empire. The mediator of this quid-pro-quo relationship was the High Priest and the temple personnel who served him, including temple scribes. First-century Jewish historian Josephus gives the following account of Antiochus's entrance into Jerusalem:

Since the Jews, upon our first entrance on their country, demonstrated their friendship towards us, and when we came into their city [Jerusalem], received us in a splendid manner, and came to meet us with their senate, and gave abundance of provisions to our soldiers, and to our elephants . . . we have determined, on account of their piety towards God, to bestow on them, as a pension, for their sacrifices of animals that are fit for sacrifice, for wine, and oil, and frankincense, the value of twenty thousand pieces of silver, and [six] sacred artabrae of fine flour, with one thousand four hundred and sixty medimni of wheat, and three hundred and seventy-five medimni of salt. . . . I would also have the work about the temple finished, and the cloisters, and if there is anything else that ought to be rebuilt . . . and let all of the nation live according to the laws of their own country; and let the senate, and the priests, and the scribes of the temple, and the sacred singers, be discharged from poll-money and the crown tax and other taxes also. And that the city may the sooner recover its inhabitants, I grant a discharge from taxes for three years to its present inhabitants, and to such as shall come to it, until the month of Hyperberetaeus. We shall also relieve them in future from a third part of their taxes, that the losses they have sustained may be repaired. And all those citizens that have been carried away, and are become slaves, we grant them and their children their freedom, and give order that their substance be restored to them. (*Antiquities*, 12.138–44)

Ben Sira's effusive eulogy for the High Priest Simon (50:1-24) and his frequent commendation of the priests and their cultic responsibilities (e.g., 34:21–35:13; 45:6-22) indicate that he was one of the educated "scribes of the temple" Josephus describes, most likely a member of the "retainer class" who served the High Priest and the ruling class.[11] In this role, he would have contributed to and benefited from cooperation with the High Priest and the Seleucid imperials, who exercised political and economic power through priestly offices. Jewish citizens recognized the authority of the High Priest by obeying cultic prescriptions (35:1-4), which in turn signaled compliance with the empire's regulatory policies. If they failed to follow cultic laws, Josephus reports, they were obligated to pay to the priests a fine of "three thousand drachmae of silver" (*Antiquities*, 12.146), a portion of which the empire would collect in taxes. As a scribe and teacher of elite students with opportunities to advance themselves in the bureaucracy of a Gentile world, Ben Sira's instructions were guided by proverbial wisdom: "if you are useful to the rich, they will work with you" (13:4), in other words, "prudent people will please the powerful" (20:28). Both teacher and student made their living by serving the bureaucracy.[12]

A commercialized loyalty—political generosity in return for social compliance—constitutes the *ethos* for an "*ethics* [from the same Greek word, *ēthos*] of caution."[13] As one commentator observes, "The person who aspires to serve the great, as Ben Sira does, is not well positioned for the role of social critic."[14] Wholehearted embrace of Greek values risks the loss of Jewish identity. Thoughtless opposition, however, triggers retaliation that threatens survival. Compromise is the better course of wisdom. "Take care" how you act in the presence of powerful people, Ben Sira advises, mistakes can be humiliating:

> *Take care* [*hišāmēr*] that you don't go astray,
>> and don't be humiliated by your own foolishness.
> When powerful people invite you,
>> show yourself reluctant,
>> and they will invite you all the more.
> Don't be forward, or you might be rejected;
>> and don't stand far off, or you might be forgotten.
> Don't think that you can speak with them as an equal,
>> and don't trust in their lengthy conversations,
>>> because they will test you with a lot of talking;
>>> and when they are smiling, they are really examining you.
> Those who won't guard your secrets are cruel,
>> and they won't spare you from mistreatment and oppression.
> *Be on guard* [*hišāmēr*] and pay attention,
>> because you are tiptoeing around your own downfall.
>> (13:8-13 emphasis added)

The counsel of caution extends through virtually all of Ben Sira's instructions on both practical and religious matters.

Dining with the rich:

Have you been seated at a magnificent table?
> Don't be greedy as you sit there, and don't say,
> "Look how much food there is!"

Remember, a greedy eye is a bad thing. . . .

Don't reach out your hand for whatever you see,
> and don't crowd your dinner companion by reaching into the same
> bowl.

Put yourself in your companion's place,
> and be considerate in everything.

Eat what's put in front of you like a normal human being,
> and don't chew rudely, or you will be hated.

Be the first to stop, to show your good breeding,
> and don't be gluttonous; otherwise, you will offend.

If you have been seated with a lot of people,
> don't help yourself before they do. (31:12-18)

Honor and respect for parents:

My child, help your father in his old age,
> and don't give him grief during his life.

And if his understanding fails,
> be tolerant, and don't shame him,
> because you have all your faculties.

Taking care of one's father won't be forgotten.
> It will be credited to you against your sins. (3:12-14; cf. 7:27-28)

Contentment and greed:

Be content with a little or a lot,
> and you will never be put down for being a sojourner.

Going from house to house is a miserable life,
> and wherever you are an immigrant, don't open your mouth. (29:23-24)

Dealing with friends and enemies:

> When people are prosperous,
>> their enemies are in pain,
>
> and when they meet with adversity,
>> even friends will keep away.
>
> Don't ever trust your enemies;
>> for just as copper corrodes,
>
>> so their wickedness does as well. . . .
>
> Don't put them next to you;
>> they might overthrow you and take your place.
>
> Don's sit them on your right side,
>> since they might take your seat. (12:9-10, 12)

Of particular importance in Hellenic society is conformity to social and moral conventions, which preserves one's honor and avoids public disgrace. In the *Illiad*, for example, Homer depicts the fractured relationship between the Trojans and the Achaeans as the result of Agamemnon's dishonorable behavior and the shame it caused Achilles. Ben Sira is similarly concerned that his students guard their reputations, because a good name is better than a thousand treasures of gold (41:12-13; cf. Eccl 7:1). He urges them to distinguish between conduct that brings shame and conduct that brings and sustains honor (4:23). The section titled "Instruction about Shame" (41:14a)[15] is a good example. The first half of the poem focuses on conduct that is shameful, including repeated cautions about sexual sins:

> Be ashamed:
>> of sexual immorality before your father and mother,
>> of lying before a prince or leader,
>> of error before a judge and an official,
>> of lawlessness before the assembly and the people,
>> of injustice before a partner and friend,
>> of theft in the neighborhood where you are staying.
>
> Be ashamed:
>> before the Lord's truth and covenant,
>> of leaning on your elbow at meals,

of showing contempt when receiving or giving,
of silence when people greet you,
of looking at a female escort,
of turning away a relative,
of depriving someone of a share or a gift,
of staring at another man's wife,
of fooling around with his female servant—
    (and don't get near her bed),
of reproachful words before friends (and don't criticize after you give),
of repeating gossip;
and of revealing secrets—

then you will be truly modest and find favor with every human being.
    (41:17–42:1a; cf. 3:1-6; 4:20-31; 10:19-25; 20:21-23)

The second half of the poem accents ethical behavior that is not shameful, behavior that should characterize one whose honor is defined by obedience to the Mosaic covenant:

Don't be ashamed of these things,
    and don't show favoritism so that you sin.

Don't be ashamed:
of the Law of the Most High or the covenant,
of a just verdict in favor of an ungodly person,
of keeping a record of expenses with a partner or a traveling companion,
of distributing an inheritance to others,
of accuracy with scales and weights,
of acquiring a lot or a little,
of profit from business with merchants,
of frequent discipline of children,
and of whipping wicked household slaves until they bleed.

In the case of a wicked wife,
    using your seal on your documents and supplies is a good idea,
    and lock up things anywhere there are lots of hands.

Whatever you deposit, whether by number or weight,
    and whatever you receive, put everything in writing.

110

> Don't be ashamed of discipline for the stupid and foolish
>> and for the old codger who is guilty of sexual immorality.
>
>> Then you will have been truly educated and approved by everyone alive.
>> (42:1b-8)

Ben Sira's ethics of caution aspires *both* to gain the approval of everyone in Hellenic Judah (42:1a, 8)—Seleucid rulers and fellow Jews alike—*and* to summon Jews to obey the "Law of the Most High [God]" (42:8). To meet this challenge, he exploits Seleucid tolerance for limited Jewish autonomy by crafting a form of submission that satisfies *both* the political obligations of the Jews to their civil rulers *and* their religious commitments to God. In Socratic fashion, he asks questions that lead his students to the contextualized (Hellenized) truth he would have them learn:

Question: "What offspring are honorable?"

Answer: "Those who fear the Lord."

Question: "What offspring are dishonorable?"

Answer: "Those who violate the commandments."

Conclusion: The official, the judge, and the ruler will be glorified,
but none of them are greater than the one who fears the Lord.
(10:19, 24)

At the heart of Ben Sira's wisdom is counsel that is common in colonized settings: "Give to Caesar what belongs to Caesar and to God what belongs to God" (Matt 22:21 and parallels: Mark 12:17; Luke 20:25; cf. Rom 13:7; 1 Pet 2:17). The key to Ben Sira's understanding of how such cautious delineations are to be made lies in the new synthesis he forges between fear of God, wisdom, and Law.[16]

Fear of God, Wisdom, and Law: The Ethics of Submission

Ben Sira was not the first sage to associate wisdom with the fear of God, as we have seen in previous discussions of Proverbs, Job, and

Ecclesiastes; nor was he the first to make a connection between wisdom and the Law, which is already present in Deuteronomy's account of Moses's address to the Israelites at Mount Horeb (Deut 4:5-6; cf. Ezra 7:25). He did, however, construct a correlation between these three aspects of sapiential instruction that represents a significant transformation in ancient Israel's understanding of the nature and purpose of intellectual inquiry. Much of what he contributes to this transformation has to do with instructions concerning the Law, which we will address below, but first it is important to note subtle but substantive developments in his presentation of the relationship between wisdom and the fear of God.

A series of poems throughout the book accents Ben Sira's views on wisdom (1:1-10; 4:11-19; 6:18-37; 14:20–15:10; 24:1-22). The opening poem in 1:1-10 asserts that God is the source of all wisdom and the only One who knows wisdom's expanse, which is as limitless as eternity itself. This affirmation echoes what is already found in Proverbs 8 and Job 28, but Ben Sira goes further by declaring that God makes wisdom available in different measures and in different ways. God "pours out" (*chorēgeō*, 1:9b) wisdom on all of creation, but "to those who love him," God "pours out" (*chorēgeō*, 1:10b) wisdom still more abundantly.[17] The poem in chapter 24 extends and develops the idea of a distinction between the universal wisdom God gives to all and the particular wisdom God bestows on the "glorified people" of Israel, "the people the Lord chose for his inheritance" (24:12).

> I [Wisdom] came forth from the mouth of the Most High,
>> and I covered the earth like a mist. . . .
>
> I sought a resting place among all of these [every people and nation, v. 6].
>> In whose allotted territory should I make my home?
>
> Then the creator of all things gave me a command;
>> the one who created me pitched my tent
>> and said, "Make your dwelling in Jacob, and let Israel receive your
>>> inheritance." . . .
>
> I ministered before him in the holy tent,
>> and so I was established in Zion.
>
> In the same way, he made the dearly loved city my resting place
>> and established my authority in Jerusalem. (24:3, 7-8, 10-11)[18]

Sirach 1:8 makes only a passing reference to wisdom and the fear associated with God: "There is one who is wise, greatly feared, seated upon his throne." The poem that immediately follows (1:11-30) makes the connection explicit:

> Wisdom starts with fearing the Lord. . . .
>
> Wisdom is fully satisfied with fearing the Lord. . . .
>
> Fearing the Lord is Wisdom's crowning garland. . . .
>
> Fearing the Lord is Wisdom's root. . . .
>
> Fearing the Lord brings wisdom and education (1:14, 16, 18, 20, 27; cf. 19:20a; 21:11b)

Ben Sira essentially reiterates an aspect of wisdom—"fear of the LORD"—that has been prominent in older wisdom texts (note especially Prov 1:7; 9:10; 15:33; Job 28:28). But here again, he expands conventional sapiential rhetoric with the most detailed discussion in wisdom literature of the linkage between the fear of the Lord, wisdom, and obedience to the Law. The grandson's prologue announces at the outset that this synthesis is a major theme in the book (13-14, 34-35). Ben Sira himself previews the theme in 1:26-27—"If you want to find Wisdom, then keep her commandments, and the Lord will supply her to you in vast quantities. Fearing the Lord brings wisdom and education"—and returns to it repeatedly in subsequent lessons (e.g., 6:32-37; 15:1; 19:20; 21:11; 23:17, 27). The pivotal discussion occurs in chapter 24, the centerpiece of the book.

Sirach 24 divides into three units: vv. 1-22, a first-person speech by personified Wisdom in praise of herself; vv. 23-29, a third-person narrative describing Wisdom's relationship to the Law; and vv. 30-34, a first-person speech by Ben Sira describing his relationship to Wisdom and the Law. The key to the synthesis Ben Sira constructs lies in the opening lines of section two. A literal rendering accents the critical issues:

"All these things [*tauta panta*] _____the book of the covenant of the Most High God [*biblios diathēkēs theou uphistou*]

the Law that Moses commanded us [*nomon on eneteilato ēmin Mōusēs*]" (v. 23)

The antecedent of "All these things" is ambiguous, but the context suggests the reference is to all that Wisdom has said in the preceding verses about her relationship to God and to Israel: "I came forth from the mouth of the Most High. . . . I took root in a glorified people [Israel]. . . . Come to me" (vv. 3, 12, 19). "All these things" about Wisdom are now juxtaposed with "the book of the covenant of the Most High God," a phrase taken from Exodus 24:7, and with "the Law that Moses commanded us," a verbatim quote from Deuteronomy 33:4. Ben Sira clearly makes a connection between Wisdom and Law, the latter conceived as both the commandments (laws) given to Moses at Sinai and the broader narrative contained in the Pentateuch (the Torah), but the omission of a verb in the first line leaves the nature of this connection unclear. The simplest grammatical solution is to supply the verb "is": Wisdom *is* the book of the covenant/Law.[19] Recent commentators have argued for a more nuanced "correlation" between Wisdom and Torah, not a strict equivalence.[20] By either reading, however, Ben Sira introduces the Law into Israel's wisdom tradition in an unprecedented way. In the words of one commentator: "Ben Sira makes an astonishing statement . . . access to wisdom comes through reflection on the divine commandments, no longer through studying human nature and human experience, as maintained in Proverbs, the book of Job, and Ecclesiastes."[21]

Having coupled Wisdom and Law together, Ben Sira proceeds to compare Wisdom/Law to the cosmic waters that flow out of Eden to the outermost parts of creation and to the Nile and Jordan rivers, which fertilize Egypt and Jordan (vv. 25-27; cf. Gen 2:10-14). Eden provides the setting for the futility of the human quest to "know wisdom completely," a limitation shared by everyone, from "the first human" to the "last" (vv. 28-29). Ben Sira's understanding of God's purpose in creating human beings with innate limitations receives further comment in 17:1-14. God gave human beings the capacity to think and reason, even to know (*epistamai*, vv. 7a, 11a) good and evil, *and* God simultaneously placed the fear of God into their hearts.[22] Both assertions rewrite the creation accounts in Genesis 1–2 by embedding wisdom and piety into God's primordial plan for human beings. The God-given capacities of mind and heart, however, are not primarily instruments for acquiring knowledge about the mysteries of life that so concerned Job and Qohelet. Instead, God puts fear into human hearts and minds so that they may praise God's glory and majesty and obey the "eternal covenant" that provides the code for ethical behavior (vv. 9-14; see further, below). "This is the end of the matter," Qohelet's epilogist concludes, "Worship God and keep God's commandments because this is what everyone must do" (Eccl 12:13). Ben Sira concurs, "Fearing the Lord is the whole of wisdom, and all wisdom involves doing the Law" (19:20).

The third section of Sirach 24 (vv. 30-34) returns to first-person speech, using the same pronoun, "I" (*egō*, v. 30), to introduce Ben Sira's words that began and concluded Wisdom's words in the first section (vv. 3, 16). Having just described the futility of humans to grasp the Wisdom/ Law that flows out of Eden's rivers, Ben Sira now rhetorically steps into the garden with a self-anointed "I" that mirrors Wisdom's "I": "*I'll* water *my* garden, and *I'll* drench *my* flower bed. . . . The canal turned into a river *for me*, and *my* river turned into a sea" (vv. 30-31, emphasis added). The inference is not only that Ben Sira understands himself as the rightful owner of Wisdom's garden and as such the one whom Wisdom serves, but also that Ben Sira himself personifies wisdom.[23] He "pours out" instructions like the rivers of Wisdom/Law that overflow the banks of the Tigris (cf. vv. 25, 33). Wisdom/Law "shines forth" education like light (v. 25); Ben Sira's instructions "shine forth" like the dawn that announces new beginnings (v. 32).

He demurs from hubris by declaring that his work is selfless, not self-serving (v. 34), but his final words in the book seem to reiterate the claim that his "I" has merged with, perhaps even subordinated, Wisdom's "I": "*I* asked for her [Wisdom]"; "*I* will search for her"; "*I* chased her down"; "*I* received her;" "*I* made progress with her" (51:14-17 emphasis added; cf. 50:27-29). When he summons his students to submit to the yoke of Wisdom's instructions (51:26), he essentially rephrases the invitation to submit to his own wisdom: "Draw near to *me*, you who lack education, and stay in *my school*" (51:23 emphasis added). If fearing the Lord is the whole of wisdom, and if all wisdom involves obedience to the Law, then an ethic of subordination to authority—God's, Wisdom's, the Law's, Ben Sira's, and, by extension, Judah's Seleucid rulers—is the core of Ben Sira's message.

In keeping with the sapiential tradition's interest in intellectual inquiry, students of Ben Sira may reflect on the wisdom of embracing his understanding of the ethos and ethics of submission. Submission to authority requires relinquishing independence and autonomy. In the political world of Ben Sira's Judah submission to Seleucid control is the price paid for survival and the promise of reasonable prosperity. Consent provides security and circumscribes discontent; it signals a readiness to accept what is given by the empire, an agreement not to ask or demand more than has been allotted. "Don't follow your inclination or your strength, in order to walk in the desires of your heart" (5:2), Ben Sira warns his students; learn instead how to serve those who are in power (8:8). Political power can be abusive, in which case compliance signals cowardice and a refusal to contest injustice, but so long as the benefits of obedience outweigh the costs of resistance, Ben Sira's ethic of caution may be persuasive.

Ben Sira's status as a member of the "retainer class" that serves the High Priest and the governing elite depends on persuading his students that political compliance entails a corresponding intellectual caution. The search for wisdom, the desire to know more about God and the way the world works, requires the subordination of autonomous inquiry to fear of God and obedience to the Law. God gives commandments that reveal divine wisdom; humans do not construct them based on experience or insight. Commandments require unarguable obedience; they are not subject to discussion or debate. As a matter of practice, both prophets and priests typically evoke obedience to the Law when dissent threatens to subvert God's covenantal relationship with Israel. Ben Sira's summons to a wisdom centered in submission to God's will responds to the dissent within the wisdom tradition represented by Job and Qohelet, a dissent he sees as a threat within in his own community.

> Don't seek out things that are too difficult for you,
>> and don't investigate matters too perplexing for you.
> Think about what you have been commanded,
>> because you have no need for matters that are hidden.
> Don't meddle in things beyond your own affairs
>> since you have already been shown things beyond human
>> understanding.

Speculation has led many people astray,
>   and false conjectures have weakened their thoughts. (3:21-24)

He [God] has given no one the power to proclaim his works.
>   Who can search out his majestic deeds? . . .
>   It's impossible to search out the wonders of the Lord.
When people finish, then they are just beginning,
>   and when they pause, then they are puzzled. (18:4, 6b-7)

It's not for us to say,
>   "What's this?" or "For what purpose is that?"
>   Everything will be examined at its proper time. (39:17; cf. vv. 21, 34)

By bringing the sapiential tradition into alignment with the Law, Ben Sira directs it away from the open inquiry that lies at the heart of international wisdom. Wisdom begins not with curiosity about the unknown but instead with gratitude for what God has revealed. Its objective is not to search for truth or expand human knowledge but to evoke awe, wonder, and praise of God. One attains this kind of wisdom not by questioning the unquestionable but by yielding to divine truth that exceeds comprehension. Ben Sira's understanding of wisdom brings it into conformity with the emphasis on covenantal obedience that predominates in the Law and the Prophets. When it comes to affirming the importance of obedience to God, the Law, the Prophets, and the Writings essentially speak with one voice. Ben Sira's students may ask, however, if the benefits of orthodoxy outweigh the loss of independent and unrestricted thinking. Is wisdom that preempts or limits or discourages the endless pursuit of knowledge still wisdom, or is it only a strategy for securing conformity to what is given, an indifference to what might be?

Ben Sira's God: "The Lord Is the All"

Ben Sira, like all sages, is a teacher of wisdom; and like all teachers, he uses a variety of rhetorical styles to communicate his lessons. One of his preferred forms of address is the didactic hymn of praise, examples of which occur repeatedly throughout the book.[24] The hymn in 42:15–43:33

is particularly instructive for understanding Ben Sira's ideas about the nature and character of God and the way the wise should respond. It conveys both Ben Sira's epistemology, how one knows God, and the ethical imperatives he derives from this knowledge.

The hymn is structured as a conventional song of praise (e.g., Pss 104, 148): a declaration of intent to praise the "works of God" (42:15-21); a listing of reasons for praising God; the indescribable beauty of nature (42:22–43:26); and an invitation to praise God, which in this case functions as Ben Sira's summons to his students to follow his example (43:27-33). What are his students to learn from this lesson? The teacher makes the point twice, once at the beginning, then again at the end: the transcendent wisdom of God exceeds all comprehension even as it summons those who would be wise to think about the unthinkable (42:17; 43:30).

The praise Ben Sira models emerges out of personal observation. He speaks about what he has been able to understand for himself about God; he uses his mind to think about what he has seen with his own eyes (42:15b; cf. 42:22b; 43:32b). His *method* for acquiring knowledge conforms to conventional wisdom practice, which stresses human cognition not divine revelation. His stated *purpose* for learning, however, is to praise "the splendors of his [divine] wisdom" (*ta megaleia tēs sophias autou*, 42:21), not to examine or scrutinize them, which is a sage's typical objective. From the outset, therefore, Ben Sira models for his students a wisdom focused more on piety than on intellect, more on acknowledging who God is and what God has done than on asking why things are as they are. God knows everything there is to know, everything past, present, and future; there is no wisdom that exceeds God's, no piece of information that God lacks (42:18-19). In Ben Sira's words: "Nothing can be added to him nor be taken away, and he needed no one to give him advice" (42:21).

The lesson from the first unit of Ben Sira's didactic hymn (42:15-21) is that *praising God* is the necessary response to looking upon the majesty of God. The lesson from the second unit (42:22–43:26), which surveys the expanse of the cosmos from heaven to earth to sea, is that *obedience to God* is the necessary response of everything God has created: "everything obeys [*hypakouei*] him" (42:23b).[25] Two emphases within these units merit special attention.

(1) *The moral coherence of creation depends on the delicate balance God maintains between polar opposite forces.* Ben Sira does not elaborate; he says only that "all things exist in pairs, one opposite the other, and he made nothing that was incomplete" (42:24). A somewhat fuller description occurs in 33:14-15, which functions as a summary of God's providential design for creation.

> Good is the opposite of evil, and life is the opposite of death;
>> so the sinner is the opposite of the godly.
>
> Observe, then, all the works of the Most High,
>> two by two, one opposite the other. (cf. 11:14)

The capacity of divine providence to join opposites together into a harmonious whole, into the one divine *logos*, is fundamental to Stoic philosophy. In the *Hymn to Zeus*, for example, Cleanthes (331–232 BCE), the Stoic philosopher who succeeded Zeno, declares: "You have so welded into one all things good and bad that they all share in a single everlasting reason [*logon aien*]."[26] Ben Sira's view is similar. Like Zeus, who welds chaos into harmony, God is a potter (33:13) molding the disparate parts of creation into cosmic unity: "all things hold together by his word [*logo*]" (43:26b).

Why do all things exist in pairs? Why does a sovereign God choose to create both good and evil? Is such opposition necessary for God's world to be "supremely good" (Gen 1:31)? Why must humans choose between polar opposites, and why do some make wrong choices such that God decides they are to be numbered among the wicked, not the righteous? Such questions are deeply embedded in the traditions Ben Sira and his fellow sages inherited, and predecessors like Job and Qohelet vigorously addressed them. Indeed, asking such questions marks the genesis of the pursuit of wisdom, as ancient Israel's primordial creation accounts confirm. Having placed humans in a paradisiacal garden, God proscribed their access to knowledge of good and evil, lest they attain wisdom by their own means (Gen 2:16; 3:16). The serpent, "the most intelligent" of God's creatures, asks the first of what would be many questions in the Old

Testament about why God does what God does: "Did God really say that you shouldn't eat from any tree in the garden?" (Gen 3:1).[27]

Ben Sira is clearly aware of these questions, and his "doctrine" of God enables him to craft his own careful (cautious) way of dealing with them—or displacing them. He asserts settled conclusions:

- God put life and death before every person and leaves the decision about which to choose to them: "He doesn't command anyone to be ungodly" (15:11-20).

- God places aspects of divinity in every human being—they are created in God's image—including the ability to think and reason: "God gave them the capacity to plan, a tongue and eyes, ears and a mind for thinking" (17:6).

- God molds human beings according to a plan that brings God pleasure:

> In the fullness of his knowledge
>> the Lord made distinctions between them,
>> and he made their ways different.
> Some of them he blessed and lifted up,
>> and some he made holy and brought them
>>> near to himself;
>> some of them he cursed, brought low, and
>> expelled them from their place.
> Like clay in the potter's hand, shaped according to the
>> potter's pleasure,
>> so are human beings in the hand of the one
>> who made them. (33:11-13; cf. 39:25-27)

- God's justice is predictably fair, equitable, and merciful: "The Lord is a judge, and he shows no partiality. . . . He repays individuals according to their deeds and the works of human beings according to their thoughts . . . [he] makes them glad by his mercy" (35:15b, 24-25).

Inconsistencies in Ben Sira's assertions invite questions from those who have "a mind for thinking"—if God has already decided to bless some and curse others, do humans really have moral agency to choose for themselves between right and wrong?—but the objective of assertions is to silence such questions.

> Don't say, "Who'll have power over me?"
>> When the Lord punishes, he will punish.
> Don't say, "Sure, I sinned, but what happened to me?" (5:3-4)
> Don't say, "I fell away because of the Lord." . . .
> Don't say, "The Lord made me go astray." (15:11-12)
>
> It's not for us to say,
>> "What's this?" or "For what purpose is that?" . . .
> It's not for us to say,
>> "This is worse than that." (39:17 [repeated in v. 21], 34)[28]

In sum, Ben Sira says, "All the works of the Lord are very good. Every command of his will be carried out in its proper time. . . . Everything will prove its worth at the proper moment. . . . Now, sing hymns with all your heart and voice, and bless the Lord's name" (39:16, 34b-35). In other words, "Be obedient, be amazed, but do not ask why."[29]

(2) *Contemplation of the beauty and wonder of creation displaces experiential and intellectual conundrums.* Ben Sira begins the hymn by declaring his intent to tell what he has learned from reflecting on "the works of the Lord" (42:15). His words echo those in 17:8, where he announces that God has attuned everyone's heart to "awe" "in order to show them the greatness of his works."[30] The vivid details of God's handiwork in 43:1-26 are an amplification of this awe. Pondering the moral coherence of God's intricately constructed world, Ben Sira says, enables one to be transformed by nature's beauty and wonder. The psalmist's hymn of praise provides a parallel discernment:

> Lord, our Lord, how majestic is your name throughout the earth!
>> You made your glory higher than heaven! . . .

> When I look up at your skies, at what your fingers made—
> the moon and the stars
> that you set firmly in place—
>   what are human beings that you think about them;
>   what are human beings that you pay attention to them? (Ps 8:1,
>   3-4; cf. Ps 144:3-4; Job 7:17-18)

Ben Sira ponders the heights of the heavens, the cycles of the sun and the moon, and the stars and rainbows and clouds that ornament the sky. He considers the phenomena that transform earth's environment: thunder and lightning, snow and ice and frost, mist and dew. He lingers on details: the heat of the sun that burns like a furnace and breathes out fire; clouds that march across the sky like armies; snow that flies like birds and settles on the land like locusts. The systematic listing of the elements and the careful observance of their individual characteristics is of itself the model of the disciplined—one might even say, "scientific"—examination expected from a sage.[31]

Immersion in the details of creation's splendor is not, however, an intellectual exercise for Ben Sira, as the third unit in the hymn makes clear (43:27-33). The objective is not to convey information attained by rational inquiry but instead to evoke in his students a wonder that surpasses comprehension. When they shift their attention away from asking *why* things are as they are and consider instead the "incredible and amazing" (*paradoxa kai thaumasia*, 43:25, literally, "beyond glory and wonder") work that God has done, their questions will transform into expressions of wonder:

> Where will we find the strength to glorify him? (43:28a)

> Who has seen him and will describe him?
> Whose praises of him will match what he really is? (43:31)

Like the psalmist, they will be overwhelmed by the One whose dominance is "awesome" and "very great" and "marvelous" (*thaumastē*, 43:29, literally, "wonder-full"). They will recognize that they cannot grasp even a fraction of who God is and what God does (43:32). They will bow in humble obedience (cf. 42:23) to the mystery and majesty of God. Every unknown—all questions and uncertainties—will recede before one "final word": "The Lord is 'the All'" (*To pan estin autos*, 43:27). As one commentator puts it, "All of creation as a whole and in each of its parts cannot be explained except through God, who is the source and abiding sustainer of all."[32]

To assert the unbridgeable chasm between the infinite and the finite, the eternal and the temporal, may be all that needs be said to convince Ben Sira's students that God's grandeur always exceeds human wisdom. The psalmist's response may have orthodoxy's stamp of approval: in the presence of such an awesome God, human beings should bow in humility, then rise to offer thanks and praise. Ben Sira would likely have known, however, that Job had carefully considered the psalmist's words and had found them utterly unconvincing. Job saw the same skies the psalmist had seen; he spoke the same words the psalmist had spoken (Job 7:17), but the view from the ash heap of inexplicable brokenness and loss—seven sons and three daughters dead, by God's own admission, "for no reason" (Job 2:3)—was grotesquely different. It demanded protest not praise, relentless questions about God's justice not bowed submission to pious assertions that Job's personal experience so definitively falsified.

Ben Sira would also have known that when Job's three friends failed to silence his questions with conventional arguments, a fourth friend, Elihu, made another attempt using a different strategy. He employed a didactic hymn (36:26–37:13) in praise of nature's moral cohesion in an effort to shift Job's attention away from the chaos that wrecked his life.

> Look, God is exalted and unknowable;
> > the number of his years is beyond counting. . . .
> Whether for punishment, for his world, or for kindness,
> > God makes it all happen.
> Hear this, Job;
> > stop and ponder God's mighty deeds. (Job 36:26; 37:13-14)

Elihu's hymn was very likely the model for Ben Sira.[33] He would have known that Elihu, whose eloquence mirrored that of God himself in the whirlwind speeches (38:1–40:2; 40:6–41:34), was nonetheless no more effective in shifting Job away from unbridled argumentation and toward obligated awe than the three friends. At the end of the divine speeches, Job declares that he has come to a new understanding of "wonders beyond my comprehension" (42:3). The new knowledge derives from both what God has revealed to him and what he has seen and heard for himself—"My ears had heard about you [God], but now my eyes have seen you. Therefore I . . ." (42:5-6a)—but the substance of what he has learned is far from clear.[34] In the trajectory of the wisdom tradition, Ben Sira speaks as if he were Job's fifth friend—"Now . . . *I'll* tell about what *I've* seen" (Sir 42:15; emphasis added)—the one who can bring the debate to its intended conclusion in a way Eliphaz, Bildad, Zophar, and Elihu (and God) could not.

All those whose claim to wisdom inspires them to believe they have the final say on any matter should expect to be challenged. Ben Sira's conversation partners do not speak in the book, but his repeated attempts to preempt their contribution ("Don't say . . .") betray their presence. Contemporary students of Ben Sira have nevertheless raised questions that resist finalization. I appropriate two, with brief comment, in the interest of sustaining the search for wisdom.[35]

(1) What is the moral and ethical significance of cultivating a sense of wonder as *a* or *the* way to wisdom? The question is central in the discussion about knowledge between Socrates and his student Theaetetus. The student has proposed one definition of knowledge after another, each one vulnerable to Socrates's critique. As a result, Theaetetus finds himself lost in wonder (*thaumazein*); knowledge must be sought, but it cannot be found. Socrates responds, "This is an experience which is characteristic of a philosopher, this wondering [*thaumazein*]: this is where philosophy begins and nowhere else" (*Theaetetus,* 155d). Ben Sira stresses the virtues of understanding the search for knowledge as beginning and ending in wonder: it cultivates the discipline of focusing on something other than personal wants or needs. Objects of wonder—the shape of a cloud, the color of a flower, the gift of love, the nature of God—call us to see the essential beauty and goodness all around us that exceeds rational analysis.

And yet, while wonder can open us to the surprise of a new discovery, it can also prevent the inquiry that might lead to learning something new. Socrates cautioned Theaetetus to be wary of teachers who would use wonder as a reason not to ask questions that cannot be answered. Some teachers will "go on asking you whether it was possible to know something clearly and sometimes dimly; or to know near at hand and not from a distance; or to know the same thing both intensely and slightly." The process will continue until "you have been struck with his wisdom—that 'answer to many prayers'—and had got yourself thoroughly tied up by him. Then, when he had you *tamed* and *bound*, he would set you free for a ransom" (*Theaetetus*, 165d-e, emphasis added). Wonder that domesticates curiosity and limits inquiry can be a tool for leveraging power, secular or religious, and enforcing compliance with dictums that reward resignation and penalize desire.

(2) Can a wisdom of wonder that displaces hard questions about God, world, and humankind with inscrutable assertions of the essential goodness and beauty of creation be ethically urged on those whose reality is pain and suffering? To be surprised by wonder, one must look away from what is immediate and pressing in order to gaze on what is distant and detached. Such a move can bring a different perspective, an awareness that relativizes personal experience by locating it within a broader context presumed to be normative. It also assumes an aesthetic view of suffering, essentially cloaking it in beauty and meaning that might be imagined but is not palpably real.

It is not coincidence that those who press an ethic of wonder that diverts attention from pain and suffering are typically those not trapped in a world of suffering themselves. Ben Sira enjoys the privileges of prestige and authority in Seleucid Judah. He must be cautious because he does not have complete control of his fortune, but he has resources others do not, most importantly the time and opportunity to "ponder God's mysteries" (39:7). He has the luxury of an aesthetic appreciation of wonder; it is likely that averting his attention from life's miseries in order to think deeply about nature's beauty was not very difficult for him.

We should not judge Ben Sira's wisdom unfairly, for like the sages who preceded him, he was an intellectual. Thinking about thinking, wondering about wonder was expected of sages, whether they lived in Athens or Jerusalem. Moreover, his desire to have the last word about the essence of wisdom was little different than that of his predecessors. The sages who framed the final form of Proverbs, the sage who inserted the speeches of Elihu as a belated commentary on Job, the epilogist who added his interpretation to the end of Ecclesiastes, all had aspirations to speak with such wisdom that there was nothing more to be said after they finished their work. Nonetheless, we may wonder if there is any place in wisdom for debate about wisdom after Ben Sira. Qohelet's skepticism and Job's dissent have been pushed to the margins, their relentless search for understanding more than they knew silenced, if not erased, from the canons of sapiential orthodoxy.

For Further Reading

Adams, S. L. *Wisdom in Transition: Act and Consequence in Second Temple Instructions.* JSJSup 125. Leiden: Brill, 2008.

Argall, R. A. *1 Enoch and Sirach: A Comparative Literary and Conceptual Analysis of the Themes of Revelation, Creation, and Judgment.* SBLEJL 8. Atlanta: Scholars Press, 1995.

Balla, I. *Ben Sira on Family, Gender, and Sexuality.* Berlin: Walter de Gruyter, 2011.

Beentjes, P. C. ed. *The Book of Ben Sira in Modern Research.* Berlin: Walter de Gruyter, 1997.

———. "Happy the One Who Meditates on Wisdom" (Sir. 14, 20): *Collected Essays on the Book of Ben Sira.* Leuven: Peeters, 2006.

Camp, C. *Ben Sira and the Men Who Handle Books: Gender and the Rise of Canon-Consciousness.* Sheffield, UK: Sheffield Phoenix Press, 2013.

Corley, B. *Ben Sira's Teaching on Friendship.* BJS 316. Providence, RI: BJS, 2002.

Corley, J., and V. Skemp, eds. *Intertextual Studies in Ben Sira and Tobit.* Washington, DC: Catholic Biblical Association, 2005.

Egger-Wenzel, R. ed. *Ben Sira's God: Proceedings of the International Ben Sira Conference* (Durham 2001). BZAW 321. Berlin: Walter de Gruyter, 2001.

Ellis, T. A. *Gender in the Book of Ben Sira: Divine Wisdom, Erotic Poetry, and the Garden of Eden*. BZAW 453. Berlin: Walter de Gruyter, 2013.

Goering, G. S. *Wisdom's Root Revealed: Ben Sira and the Election of Israel*. JSJSup 139. Leiden: Brill, 2009.

Gregory, B. *Like an Everlasting Signet Ring: Generosity in the Book of Ben Sira*. Berlin: Walter de Gruyter, 2010.

Liesen, J. *Full of Praise: An Exegetical Study of Sir 39, 12-35*. JSJSup 64. Leiden: Brill, 2000.

Mack, B. L. *Wisdom and Hebrew Epic: Ben Sira's Hymn in Praise of the Fathers*. Chicago: University of Chicago Press, 1985.

Martilla, M. *Foreign Nations in the Wisdom of Ben Sira: A Jewish Sage between Opposition and Assimilation*. Berlin: Walter de Gruyter, 2012.

Mulder, O. *Simon the High Priest in Sirach 50: An Exegetical Study of Simon the High Priest as Climax to the Praise of the Fathers in Ben Sira's Concept of the History of Israel*. JSJSup 78. Leiden: Brill, 2003.

Passaro, A., and G. Bellia, eds. *The Wisdom of Ben Sira: Studies on Tradition, Redaction, and Theology*. Berlin: Walter de Gruyter, 2008.

Schnabel, J. *Law and Wisdom from Ben Sira to Paul: A Tradition Historical Inquiry into the Relation of Law, Wisdom, and Ethics*. Tübingen: J.C.B. Mohr (Paul Siebeck), 1985.

Trenchard, W. C. *Ben Sira's View of Women: A Literary Analysis*. BJS 38. Chico, CA: Scholars Press, 1982.

Wright, B. G. *Praise Israel for Wisdom and Instruction: Essays on Ben Sira and Wisdom, the Letter of Aristeas and the Septuagint*. JSJSup 131. Leiden: Brill, 2008.

Chapter 5

Wisdom of Solomon

"Doing What Is Right Means Living Forever"

The long arc of wisdom's association with Solomon, which extends from Proverbs to Ecclesiastes to Sirach, reaches its apex with the book known as the Wisdom of Solomon (in the Latin tradition, the book of Wisdom). Although Solomon is never named, the author of the book assumes his persona from beginning to end. This is particularly clear in the autobiographical speeches in Wisdom 7–9, which stand at the center of the book both structurally and thematically. Reprising Solomon's search for wisdom as recounted in 1 Kings 3, the author expands on it by affirming that God granted Solomon not only "a wise and understanding mind" along with "wealth and fame" (1 Kgs 3:12-13) but also a vast range of knowledge about cosmology, astronomy, physics, biology, and botany. In sum, Wisdom's Solomon receives from God "accurate knowledge of all that is—of how the world is made and holds together, and of the forces at work in the world's essential elements" (Wis 7:17). For the first time in wisdom literature, this Solomonic sage asserts that wisdom is the way to immortality: "I knew that because of her [Wisdom], I would gain everlasting life" (8:13; cf. 15:3).

The gift of wisdom is "knowledge of the beginning, end, and middle of time" (7:18). The sage's insight provides a clue to the structure of the book, which has its own beginning, middle, and end. There is general

129

consensus concerning the three major parts—chapters 1–6, 7–9, and 10–19—but different ways to describe the movements between the parts and their thematic accents. One useful approach is to focus on the author's use of literary devices, such as the repetition of key words and phrases to mark the beginning and ending of text units, chiasms that repeat key elements of a unit in reverse order (thus an A B C . . . C B A pattern), and sequences of antithetical comparisons.

Wisdom of Solomon

Part I: The Book of Eschatological Judgment: Reward and Punishment in the Afterlife (1:1–6:21)

    A. Exhortation: Seek wisdom and justice (1:1-11)

        B. The deluded reasoning of the ungodly (1:12–2:24)

            C. The fates of the godly and the ungodly (3:1–4:20)

        B. The final judgment against the ungodly (5:1-23)

    A. Exhortation: Seek wisdom and justice (6:1-21)

Part II: The Book of Wisdom: Wisdom's Nature and Benefits (6:22–9:18)

    A. Solomon's desire for wisdom (6:22–7:22a)

        B. Solomon's praise of wisdom's nature, origin, and attributes (7:22b– 8:22)

    A. Solomon's prayer for wisdom (9:1-18)

Part III: The Book of History: The Providential Role of Wisdom in the Exodus (10:1–19:22)

    A. Introduction: Wisdom's saving power in the history from Adam to Moses (10:1-21)

B. The providential role of Wisdom in the Exodus, illustrated by seven examples contrasting God's use of nature to punish the Egyptians but spare the Israelites (11:1–19:21)

- Nile water turned into blood, but Israelites receive water in the desert (11:1-14)

- Egyptians plagued by frogs, but Israelites eat quail (16:1-4)

- Egyptians die from bites by locusts and flies, but Israelites survive bites from poisonous serpents (16:5-14)

- Egyptians punished with hail and lightning, but Israelites feed on manna that falls from heaven like snow (16:15-29)

- Egyptians are terrified by darkness, but Israelites follow a pillow of fire (17:1–18:4)

- Egyptian firstborns die, but the Israelites' are spared (18:5-25)

- Egyptians drown in the Red Sea, but the Israelites pass through the Red Sea safely (19:1-17)

C. Conclusion: Review of Wisdom's wonders in history and nature and a concluding doxology (19:18-22)

Historical and Cultural Contexts

The author of the book is widely assumed to be a Jewish sage living in Alexandria as part of the Egyptian diaspora. He speaks in the name of

Solomon, but his composition dates to the Hellenistic period, most likely between the first century BCE and the first century CE (ca. 30 BCE–50 CE), approximately one thousand years after the time of King Solomon.

Although the exact date for Wisdom's composition remains uncertain, the general sociopolitical conditions that provide the backdrop for its message are relatively clear. There had been a Jewish presence in Alexandria since the days of Alexander's conquest of the city in 331 BCE, but it was during the rule of his successors, especially the first two Ptolemies (Soter, 303–284 BCE; Philadelphus, 283–246 BCE), that a high concentration of Jews emerged. Various migrations throughout the Ptolemaic period may have swelled the numbers to approximately 180,000, perhaps one-third of the population of the city.[1] The Jews were not legal citizens of Alexandria, but they were granted some measure of autonomy with limited privileges. As resident aliens living within a Greek polis, they administered their internal affairs and lived according to their own laws and customs. They built and attended synagogues and engaged in prayer and reading Torah. Although education for laypeople would have taken place in Jewish institutions like the synagogue, where scholars and students met to study Torah, the elite might attend the Greek gymnasium, which educated students into a broad array of skills, including rhetoric and philosophy.[2] The author of Wisdom would likely have had access to such a Greek education.

The dynamics of life in Hellenistic Alexandria presented a combination of possibilities and problems for both Jews and Greeks. For the Jewish community, Hellenism held a number of attractions. As Greek was the lingua franca of society, Jews found it both necessary and productive to become fluent in the language and comfortable in the culture of the majority population. If they were to succeed in business, acquire social respect, secure the fortunes of their families, and resolve disputes with others in the body politic, they must do so as "Hellenes," that is, as acculturated Jews.[3] The acculturation extended to translating Hebrew scripture into the Greek Septuagint, which, according to the legendary story of Aristeas, was a response to a request from Ptolemy II Philadelphus for a Greek copy of the laws of the Jews for the royal library in Alexandria.[4]

Coupled to Hellenism's appeal, however, was an intractable problem: how much could Jews accommodate themselves to Greek culture before losing their distinctive identity as Jews? When does acculturation cross the line into full-scale assimilation? The issue is clearly a concern for the author of Wisdom, whose defense of Judaism encourages those who were tempted to embrace Hellenism and abandon their heritage. So, for example, the sage's opening exhortation, addressed putatively to pagan rulers but implicitly to any who may doubt the wisdom of fidelity to God: "Love what is right. Set your mind on the Lord in goodness. Seek him with a sincere heart. Those who don't put the Lord to the test will find him. He makes himself known to those who trust him. Perverse reasoning separates people from God. His power exposes the foolish people who test him" (Wis 1:1-3). Similarly, the sage's promise that those who persevere in faith will receive the reward of the righteous: "Those who do the right thing live forever. Their reward comes from the Lord. The Most High takes care of them. For this reason, they will receive a lovely palace and a beautiful royal crown from the Lord himself. With his right hand he shelters them and with his right arm he protects them" (5:15-16).

Greeks in Alexandria were often suspicious of Jews, sometimes hostile to their very existence. They viewed Jewish refusal to worship Greek gods as both unsocial and disrespectful of their customs and values. A question posed by the Greek sophist Apion (ca. 30 BCE–45 CE) voices a common concern: "Why then, if they are citizens [*cives*], do they not worship the same gods as the Alexandrians?"[5] Greeks viewed Sabbath observance, circumcision, abstention from pork, and other such Jewish practices as superstitious folly.[6] More serious was Apion's allegation that Jews annually engaged in the ritual murder of a Greek,[7] which fueled the charge that Jews were "atheists and misanthropes."[8] Although such criticism was relatively common, it likely was more rhetoric than actualized hostility for most of the Hellenistic period. It reflected nevertheless a "Judeophobia,"[9] a deep fear turned toward hatred of the Jews that would fuel the first pogrom in Jewish history led by the Roman emperor Caligula, who unleashed his forces against the Jews in Alexandria in 38 CE. Philo gives the most detailed account of the brutal event.

Poor wretches, they [the Jews] were at once seized by those who wielded the weapon of mob rule, treacherously stabbed, dragged through the whole city, and trampled on, and thus completely made away with till not a part of them was left which could receive the burial which is the right of all. Multitudes of others also were laid low and destroyed with manifold forms of maltreatment, put in practice to serve their bitter cruelty by those whom savagery had maddened and transformed into the nature of wild beasts; for any Jews who showed themselves anywhere, they stoned or knocked out with clubs, aiming their blows at first against the less vital parts for fear that a speedier death might give a speedier release from their anguish.

Some . . . took the most effective at all, fire and steel, and slew many with the sword, while not a few they destroyed with fire. Indeed, whole families, husbands with their wives, infant children with their parents, were burnt in the heart of the city. . . . And when they lacked wood for fire they would collect brushwood and dispatch them with smoke rather than fire, thus contriving a more pitiable and lingering death for the miserable victims whose bodies lay promiscuously half-burnt. . . .

Many also while still alive they drew with one of the feet tied at the ankle and meanwhile leapt upon them and pounded them to pieces. And when by the cruel death thus devised, their life ended, the rage of their enemies did not end, but continued all the same. They inflicted worse outrages on the bodies, dragging them through almost every lane of the city until the corpses, their skin, flesh and muscles shattered by the unevenness and roughness of the ground, and all the parts united to make the organism dissevered and dispersed in different directions were wasted to nothing.[10]

Strong arguments have been advanced in support of understanding this violence toward Jews in 38 CE as the principal setting for Wisdom.[11]

Against a background of such cruelty, the sage's description of the twisted reasoning the ungodly use to justify their abuse of the Jews takes on a particular resonance:

Let's lie in ambush for the one who does what is right. He's a nuisance to us. He always opposes our actions. He blames us because we have failed to keep the Law. He condemns us for turning our backs on our upbringing. He boasts of his knowledge of God. He even calls himself the Lord's servant. He exposes our secret plans. Just to look at him makes us sick. His life isn't like the lives of others. His ways are completely different.

He thinks we're frauds. He avoids us and our actions as though we're unclean. Instead, he blesses the final days of those who do what's right. He even boasts that God is his Father.

Let's see if his words are true. Let's put him to the extreme test and see what happens. If this man who does the right thing is indeed God's son, then God will assist him. God will rescue him from the hand of those who oppress him. Let's test him by assaulting and torturing him. Then we will know just how good he really is. Let's test his ability to endure pain. Let's condemn him to a disgraceful death: according to him, God should show up to protect him. (2:12-20)

Intellectual Economy

Alexandria was a major academic center in the Hellenistic period, along with Rome, Athens, and Antioch. Greek, Egyptian, and Jewish scholars both shaped and were shaped by an intellectual economy fueled by robust discussion and debate about the major philosophical and religious ideas of the day. In the gymnasia, philosophers educated students who could pay tuition in Greek grammar, rhetoric, and composition. In the wider marketplace of ideas, itinerant sophists offered public lectures and private tutoring for those who could not afford a gymnasium education. Temples, synagogues, and state cults provided instruction in religious tradition, interpretation, and practice. The author of Wisdom would have been an active participant in this thickly variegated educational delivery system. Multiple indicators throughout the book betray a synthesis of Greek, Egyptian, and Jewish influence.

Greek Influence

Wisdom's sage not only wrote in Greek but also drew upon a variety of Greek literary features and philosophical ideas. Most prominent among the literary features is the author's adaptation of an exhortatory form of discourse the Greeks called *logos protreptikos*, a combination of rhetoric and philosophy that attempts to persuade people to a particular course of speech or action that is just, honorable, and beneficial. The form originated with the Sophists, but the best early illustration of its structure and style is

Aristotle's *Protrepticus*, which begins by exhorting people to "exercise moral virtue for the sake of wisdom, for wisdom is the supreme end" (B 21; cf. Wis 6:15) and ends by asserting that "reason is the god in us" and "mortal life contains a portion of some god" (B 110; cf. Wis 2:23; 7:25-27).[12]

Protreptic rhetoric is a common feature in Greek texts that takes a basic form: prologue, narrative, argument, counterargument, and epilogue. Each of these elements occurs in Wisdom, although not in an exact order.

- Prologue: the general exhortation to justice (1:1-15)

- Narrative: the history of the exodus (11:2–19:22)

- Argument/Counterargument: scattered throughout the book (e.g., 1:16–2:24)

- Epilogue: briefly stated in a concluding doxology (19:22)[13]

Scattered throughout this basic form are other types of Greek rhetoric that also occur in Wisdom, including:

- *enkōmion*, praise of a person or a thing (e.g., the eulogy to Wisdom's salvific role in history from Adam to Moses; 10:1–11:1)

- *synkrisis*, comparison of opposites (e.g., the contrast between God's use of nature to protect Israel and punish Egypt; 11:6–19:17)

- *prosōpopoiia*, putting imaginary speeches into the mouths (literally, on the "face," *prosópon*) of another (e.g., the speeches attributed to the ungodly; 1:16–2:20)

- *periautologia*, self-praise (e.g., Solomon's discourse on his successful quest for wisdom; chapters 7–9)

Wisdom's author uses these rhetorical features as literary vehicles for conveying ideas drawn from a variety of popular Hellenistic philosophical traditions, including Stoicism, Epicureanism, and Neopythagoreanism. The four cardinal virtues in Wis 8:7, for example—moderation, prudence (practical wisdom), justice (what is right), and courage—occur also in Plato, Stoicism, and Philo.[14] Wisdom's description of the wicked who live for the pleasures of the moment in a world where all is subject to chance is typical of an Epicurean worldview. So for example:

> And the seeds of things themselves of their own accord, jostling from time to time by chance, were driven together in the many ways, rashly, and in vain, at last those united, which, suddenly cast together, might become ever and anon the beginnings of great things, of earth and sea and sky, and the race of all living creatures. (Lucretius, 2.1-58)

> All of us came into being by chance. When our lives are over, it will be just as if we had never been. The breath in our nostrils is mere smoke. Reason is just a spark in the beating of our hearts. When that spark is extinguished, the body will be turned into ashes. The spirit will evaporate into thin air. Over time, our names will be forgotten. No one will remember our deeds. Our lives will pass away like the last wisps of a cloud. Our lives will be dispersed like a morning mist chased away by the sun and weighed down by the day's heat. Our time here is like a shadow passing by. There's no turning back from death. It has been sealed, and no one will alter it. (Wis 2:2-5)

The idea embedded in this cosmology—"reason is just a spark in the beating of our hearts"—is characteristic of Stoicism, for example, in Seneca's consideration of a theory that tries to prove that "man is part of the divine spirit, that some part, sparks, as it were, of the stars fell down to earth and lingered there in a place that is not their own" (*De Otio*, 5.5).[15] Wisdom also borrows, in a more limited way, from Neopythagoreanism— the order and harmony present in numbers (11:20b); music as a metaphor for the mystical harmony of the universe (19:18); and divine revelation as the source of philosophy or wisdom (7–9).[16]

Wisdom's author was familiar with a wide range of intellectual thought in Hellenistic Greece, as the references in the paragraphs above indicate. There is consensus, however, that the primary background for many of the key ideas in the book is Middle Platonism (ca. 80 BCE–250 CE), which represented a modernizing of the nucleus of Platonic doctrine, now blended with Stoic ethics, Aristotelian logic, and Neopythagorean metaphysics. There was considerable diversity of thought in such an eclectic philosophical mix, but a number of core beliefs were held in common, aspects of which figure prominently in Wisdom. A brief listing will suffice here; discussion will follow in the next section.

- Belief in One Supreme Being (the blending of Plato's "Good" with Aristotle's Supreme Mind or Unmoved Mover). See the description of wisdom as the cosmic principle that "holds everything together," independent of God, derived from God, and the means of God's presence in creation.

The Lord's Spirit fills the whole world. It holds everything together and knows what everyone says. (1:7)

Wisdom is the warm breath of God's power. She pours forth from the all-powerful one's pure glory. Therefore, nothing impure can enter her. She's the brightness that shines forth from eternal light. She's a mirror that flawlessly reflects God's activity. She's the perfect image of God's goodness. She can do anything, since she's one and undivided. She never changes, and yet she makes everything new. Generation after generation, she enters souls and shapes them into God's friends and prophets. God doesn't love anything as much as people who make their home with Wisdom. She's more splendid than the sun and more wonderful than the arrangement of the stars. She's even brighter than sunlight, for night follows day, but evil can never overcome Wisdom. She stands strong from one end of the world to the other. She is a marvelous governor over everything in between. (7:25–8:1)

- Distinction between body and soul:

I was a clever child and had been born with a dignified attitude—or, better said, because my soul was already dignified, it entered a spotless body. (8:19-20)

The body that is headed for destruction weighs down the soul. Our earthly container burdens our minds with cares and concerns. (9:15)

- The immortality of the soul:

The souls of those who do what is right are in God's hand. They won't feel the pain of torment. To those who don't know any better, it seems as if they have died. Their departure from this life was considered their misfortune. Their leaving us seemed to be their destruction, but in reality they are at peace. It may look to others as if they have been punished, but they have the hope of living forever. (3:1-4)

- A materialist approach to theodicy. Humans, not God, are responsible for evil:

Don't seek death through the error of your ways. Don't invite destruction on yourself by what you do. God didn't make death. God takes no delight in the ruin of anything that lives. God created everything so that it might exist. The creative forces at work in the cosmos are life-giving. There is no destructive poison in them. The underworld doesn't rule on earth. Doing what is right means living forever. (1:12-15)

- Life's goal is likeness to God, as far as is possible:

God created humans to live forever. He made them as a perfect representation of his own unique identity. (2:23)

Egyptian Influence

The intellectual ethos of Alexandria was shaped not only by Greek philosophical traditions but also by Egyptian influences, especially deeply rooted Egyptian religious values and practices. From the time of the pharaohs, Egyptian culture had been saturated with gods, temples, priests, and cultic practices that were believed to provide sustenance and security for life in both this world and the next. This culture continued to permeate Hellenized Alexandria: the names of Egyptian gods were converted to Greek ones (Amon to Zeus; Hathor to Aprodite; Horus to Apollo; Thoth to Hermes); native religions following Egyptian gods were integrated with Greek religions devoted to Zeus, Athena, Dionysus, Hermes, Pan, and Asclepius; deified pharaohs were replaced by divinized Ptolemaic rulers and their state-based cults; ancient Egyptian mythologies were embellished in Greek mystery religions that ritually reenacted the death and rebirth of particular deities. In sum, Hellenized Alexandria was a center for *both* vigorous philosophical discussion *and* vibrant religious activity. The author of the Wisdom of Solomon engaged this philosophical-religious environment as both a *critic* and a creative *recipient*.

The sage's criticisms of Egyptian religious practices are sometimes clear and straightforward; at other times, they are subtle and shaded. Wisdom 13–15 offers a three-pronged attack on Egyptian worship with a graduated assessment of the pseudo-wisdom of its practitioners.[17]

- 13:1-9 singles out two forms of nature worship: the natural elements (v. 2: fire, wind, air, water) and the celestial lights (v. 2: the "constellation of stars" and "the sky's bright lights"). The sage charges that philosophers spend time reflecting on creation's beauty but fail to discern the creator, "the maker [*technitēs*, 'artisan'] of everything" (v. 1). His conclusion: "All humans who don't know God are empty-headed by nature" (v. 1a). As one commentator puts it, they are "inherently ignorant."[18]

- 13:10–15:13 is a lengthy critique and judgment against both idol makers and idol worshippers. They make gods with their own hands out of dead things—useless stones, sawn wood— then entrust to these "lifeless images" (15:5) life's most valued treasures: marriage and children, health, wealth, security, and success (13:16-19). Such foolishness reflects more than a lack of knowledge about the true God; it is the beginning of moral depravity (14:22-26), more specifically, "the origin of all evil" (14:27). Idolaters consequently deserve a "double judgment . . . first, because they acted wickedly toward God . . . and second, because they . . . [had] contempt for what was holy" (14:30). The sage's conclusion: idolaters are more than merely foolish; they are "miserable" (*talaipōroi*, "wretched," 13:10).

- 15:14-19 brings the critique to a conclusion by moving beyond the evils of idolatry to condemn the practice of zoolatry or animal worship (cf. 11:15; 12:23-27). Those who deify stupid and brutish animals "have neither the praise nor the blessing of God" (15:19). The sage's conclusion: more than empty-headed philosophers (13:9), more than wretched idolaters (13:10), this third group of Egyptians is the "most foolish [*aphronestattoi*] of all" (15:14).

The negative critique of Ptolemaic rulers is more subtle but no less pointed. The political model for Ptolemaic rulers was derived from the pharaonic cult of divine kings in which kings were divinized heroes and saviors. On earth they embodied and actualized the gods' will; in death, mummification insured their immortality. Wisdom's author does not refer directly to any Ptolemaic ruler, but he does signal at the outset his concern about their exercise of power: "You who judge the earth, love what is right. Set your mind on the Lord in goodness. Seek him with a sincere heart" (1:1). The role model for judging the earth in accordance with divine righteousness is not the pharaonic god-king, the sage asserts indirectly, but instead Solomon, whose words he places at the center of this book of Wisdom (7–9).[19] Solomon's opening words make clear the difference between the sage's understanding of kingship and that of the Ptolemies: "I'm just a human like everyone else . . . No king has ever begun life any differently. There's only one way into life for everyone, and only one way out as well" (7:1, 5-6).

God chose Solomon to be king (9:7), which is reminiscent of pharaonic accession to the throne, but Solomon's authority comes not from innate divinity but instead from the practice of virtues taught to him by Wisdom, "the perfect image of God's goodness" who "enters souls and shapes them into God's friends and prophets" (7:26b, 27b). Wisdom's virtues are described in a series of twenty-one epithets (7:22b-23) that fall into three groups of seven (7 x 3, sacred numbers that signify perfection and completion). The first set of seven generally clusters around intelligence and purity ("insightful, holy, unique, diverse, refined, kinetic, pure"); the second set clusters around moral goodness and kindness ("spotless, transparent, harmless, delighting in what is good, sharp, unstoppable, overflowing with kindness"); the third set clusters around wisdom's ability to permeate all that exists ("delighting in humans, steadfast, secure, not anxious, all-powerful, and all-seeing"). Wisdom can teach all these virtues, and Solomon pursues them with the passion of one who has fallen in love

(8:2, 9, 16, 19; cf. Song 1:15; 2:4; 4:9-10). Wisdom's gifts to Solomon include fame and wealth (7:11), unrivalled knowledge (7:17-21), admiration among the rulers of the world (8:11-12, 14-15), and most importantly, immortality, not through pharaonic mummification but rather through a wisdom-shaped reputation that will live long after he has died: "I knew that because of her, I would gain everlasting life and that I would leave behind an everlasting memorial for those who would come after me" (8:13; by way of contrast, see the fate of the wicked in 2:2-5).

Wisdom's author did not engage Egyptian culture as only a critic who was wary of its appeal; he also embraced its creative energy and molded it to convey his own distinctive message. This is particularly true of the way he blended Isis and Sophia traditions. Isis was revered as the Egyptian goddess who rescued the dismembered body of the divine ruler Osiris and restored him to life by using her magical powers. The mythology of her power to resurrect the dead was a primary feature of the Isis cult that was one of the most popular of all in Hellenistic religions. Sophia or Wisdom is a major figure in the Book of Wisdom. She makes an initial appearance in chapter 1, dominates in chapters 6 to 10, then recedes and gradually merges with God in chapters 11 to 19.[20] The author of Wisdom did not create this figure; her presence is deeply rooted in ancient Near Eastern traditions, and she has a significant role in antecedent Jewish literature, especially in Proverbs 8, Job 28, and Sirach 24, as we have discussed in previous chapters. Wisdom's author draws upon all of these traditions and imaginatively blends them with features of Isis in order to convey his own distinctive message. One important example may be singled out.

Wisdom's author almost certainly constructs Solomon's relationship to Sophia from the model of Isis's relationship to Osiris. Sophia is the "bride" of Solomon (8:2) as Isis is the "royal spouse" of Osiris.[21] Sophia is the divine agent who secures an eternal kingship for Solomon (6:20-21) as Isis does for the Egyptian king. In reliefs at the Ptolemaic temple at Eana, Isis says to the king: "To you [I give] . . . / a long kingship for many years in peace, / for the duration of eternity and perpetuity!"[22] Moreover, Sophia is the agent by which Solomon rules (8:10-15) and attains wisdom (8:2-21), influence and power (8:12-15), and immortality (8:13,

17). Precisely the same functions are attributed to Isis. Although earlier Jewish sapiential texts attributed to Wisdom some of the same functions (e.g., Prov 8:14-21), the author of Wisdom clearly shapes his material to correspond with Isis royal ideology.

On close examination, however, it is equally clear that Wisdom's author uses the Isis traditions to introduce new features into the Jewish understanding of Wisdom's role in their particular history. For example, Isis is viewed as a "savior" who rescues her people from the throes of pain and suffering, even death, and restores them to life and prosperity. An inscription at Medinet Madi is one of several that attribute this role to Isis: "As many as are in prison . . . in pain . . . who wander in foreign lands . . . all these are saved when they pray that you [Isis] be present."[23]

Wisdom's author also presents Wisdom as a "savior" by strategically inserting her into Israel's history as recorded in Genesis and Exodus. She "kept watch over the world's first-formed parent . . . [and] delivered him from his grave misstep" (10:1); she saved Noah and his family during the flood (10:4); she preserved a blameless Abraham (10:5) and Lot, "a man who did what was right" (10:6); she "[rescued] her servants from their trials" (10:9), namely, Joseph (10:13) and the people who escaped Egyptian slavery (10:15). Wisdom's salvific role in this midrash[24] on Israel's history continues with a retelling of the exodus from Egypt, with Wisdom, the personification of God's guiding hand, replacing Moses as the central character in the story (11–19). The switch is indicated in the opening verse of this section: "She caused their works to prosper by the hand of the holy prophet" (11:1).

Wisdom's role as savior is a new feature in Jewish wisdom literature, which to this point had reserved this role for God. The author identifies Wisdom with the mythic power of Isis but without accepting the explicit Egyptian ideology surrounding her. As John Collins puts it:

> [The Wisdom of Solomon] offers Jews an alternative to Isis in the figure of Wisdom, but there is no hint here, or anywhere else in Jewish literature of the time, that Jews found the cult of Isis especially attractive or tempting. Rather, the tacit allusions to Isis are taken up into the complex picture of Wisdom to enrich it and make it more attractive and satisfying to a Hellenized readership. The allusions to Isis are not

essentially different in function from the more overt allusions to Greek philosophy: they make the figure of Wisdom intelligible by depicting it in terms that were familiar and well respected in a Hellenistic world.[25]

Jewish Influence

Wisdom's appropriation of Greek and Egyptian traditions did not signify wholesale adoption of Hellenism. The primary influence on Wisdom's author was in fact the Bible itself, albeit in Greek translation (the Septuagint). In every part of the book, the author makes extensive use of authoritative Jewish texts, ideas, and images, drawn from the Torah, Prophets, and Writings. In Part I (1:1–6:21), for example, creation and fall traditions in Genesis 1–3 provide the basis for the discussion of justice, death, and immortality (cf. Gen 1:26-28 and Wis 2:23); Isaiah 52:13–53:12 is the model for the judgment scene in Wisdom 5; and multiple psalms provide the vocabulary for the author's reflections on nature (e.g., Ps 9:23 in Wis 1:9; Ps 17:26 in Wis 6:10; Ps 44:8 in Wis 1:1a; Ps 47:15 in Wis 3:8). In Part II (6:22–9:18), the author uses Proverbs 8 and Sirach 24 as a template for Wisdom's praise and 1 Kings 3 and 2 Chronicles 1 for constructing Solomon's profile in Wisdom 9. The description in Part III (10:1–19:22) of Wisdom's role in leading Israel from Egypt and through the wilderness is a retelling of episodes in Exodus and Numbers, as noted above.[26] Wisdom's author is also familiar with Jewish texts and traditions that were not in the Septuagint but were nonetheless circulating (in Greek) in Alexandria; for example, apocalyptic traditions in the Dead Sea Scrolls (especially 4QInstruction; cf. 1 En 91–104) describing the after-death judgment of the righteous and the wicked, which are similar to the account of reward and punishment after death in Wisdom 1–5.[27]

Wisdom's author could also draw on a tradition of antecedent Hellenistic Jewish scholarship that advocated a "philosophical Judaism."[28] The second-century BCE Alexandrian intellectual Aristobulus, for example, argued that the Greek philosophers, including Socrates and Plato, borrowed ideas about the nature of God and cosmic order from Moses. Judaism was, in his opinion, the most significant of all "philosophical schools" in Alexandria.[29] The most influential of all these Jewish theologians/philosophers, especially for the author of the Book of Wisdom, was Philo of Alexandria (ca. 20 BCE–50 CE), who identified himself with the "school of Moses" (*De mutatione nominum* [*Mut.*], 223). Most of Philo's major ideas appear in Wisdom. Four may be singled out as especially important:[30]

- For both Philo and the Book of Wisdom, Sophia, or to use Philo's preferred term, Logos, is the transcendent reality that comes from God, mediates God's glory, and makes knowledge of God available to humans (Wis 7:25-26; 8:4; 9:1-2; cf. Philo, *De somniis* [*Somn.*], 2.221; *Quisrerum divinarium heres sit* [*Her.*], 199; *Quod deterius potiori insidari soleat* [*Det.*], 54).

- Both describe God as an artisan (Wis 7:22; *De opificio mundi* [*Opif.*] 15-25) who creates the world out of primordial matter (Wis 11:17; Prov 1:22) and holds it together with a pneumatic tension between the godly and the ungodly (Wis 8:1; 16:24; *De confusion linguarum* [*Conf.*], 136; *Quod Deus sit immutablis* [*Deus.,*] 35-36). Both describe God using creation as an agent of punishment of the wicked (Wis 5:17-23; *De vita Mosis* [*Mos.*], 1.96).

- Both make immortality a central feature of their message. The just live forever (Wis 5:15; *De Iosepho* [*Ios.*], 264); after death, their souls are in God's hands (Wis 3:1; *Questiones et solutions in Genesin* [*QG.*], 1.85-86; 3.11). The wicked are physically alive but spiritually dead (Wis 1:11; 3:24; *Det.*, 49; *De specialibus legibus* [*Spec.*], 1.345).

- Both attribute similar ethical principles to wisdom: the four cardinal virtues of wisdom (Wis 8:7; *Legum allegoriarum* [*Leg.*], 1.71-72) are the key to true righteousness (Wis 3:15; *Deus*, 117–18); one seeks wisdom for its own sake and external rewards will follow (Wis 7:7-11; *Her.*, 285–86); as wisdom is *philanthrōpos* (a lover of human beings), so the righteous must be humane (Wis 1:6; 7:22-23; 12:19; *QG*, 2.60; *De decalogo* [*Decal.*], 132–34).

If Wisdom's author was both a critic and a creative recipient of Greek, Egyptian, and Jewish influences in Alexandria, then we may ask if there is a discernible objective to his synthesis of philosophy and theology, of secular (pagan) and religious thinking. Was the intention to construct a more Hellenistic form of Judaism or a more Jewish form of Hellenism? Was the purpose to offer consolation and hope to Jews demoralized by persecution? If the primary setting was Caligula's pogrom of 38 CE, then the promise of an abundant life that transcends death would surely have had an audience among beleaguered Jews. Was the objective to mount a Jewish "counter-literature"[31] that fueled resistance to Ptolemaic hegemony? The fate predicted for the wicked (read Egyptians) could just as well be a summons to join forces with the Divine Warrior God and his cosmic army in the war that will defeat the ungodly. Some mixture of all of these objectives can be appropriately attributed to the author of Wisdom. One primary discernment, advanced in this book as a distinctly Jewish philosophical principle, underlies the whole: "Since God is the author both of the truths made known by revelation and of the truths made known by reason, there can be no conflict between them."[32] The words are a commentary on Philo's advocacy of a philosophical Judaism, but they apply just as well to his contemporary, the author of the Wisdom of Solomon.

Key Issues and Theological Themes

The opening chapter identifies Wisdom (*sophia*) with "spirit" (*pneuma*, 1:6; cf. v. 5, a "holy spirit" [*agion pneuma*]) for the first time in Hebrew wisdom literature. It then adds an assertion that the rest of the book is meant to confirm: "The Lord's Spirit [*pneuma kuriou*] fills the whole world. It holds everything together" (*ta panta gnōsin*, 1:7, literally, "all knowledge"). In the middle of the book, this assertion is explicated with the claim that Wisdom is the key to "unerring knowledge" (*gnōsin apseudē*, 7:17; CEB: "accurate knowledge") concerning "the beginning, end, and middle of time" (*archēn kai telos kai mesotēta chronōn*, 7:18). This all-encompassing claim for Wisdom's role in the cosmic economy provides the context for assessing key issues and theological themes. Can wisdom hold everything together? Wisdom's protreptic argues that the answer is yes.

The Righteous and the Wicked

The contrast between the righteous and the wicked and their respective destinies is the primary focus of Part I (1:1–6:21) and signals the importance the author attaches to discerning the connection between wisdom and justice that permeates the entire book. The wicked cannot think clearly, and as a consequence they do not act ethically (2:1-20). They do not know the mysteries of God and instead keep company with "the devil," who promises life but delivers only death (2:21-24). Their fate is to reap "what their evil thinking deserves" (3:10), for as the sage argues, "Those who have contempt for wisdom and instruction . . . have no hope" (3:11). When the final judgment comes, the wicked are consumed in anguished but unrequited regret (5:6-7). The cosmos itself lends its forces to their defeat (5:20b-23). From the sage's perspective, the fate of the wicked is so unambiguously clear, that were they in a court of law, they would testify against themselves (5:3-13).

The righteous do not speak for themselves, but their attributes goad the wicked to flatter them with sarcasm that discloses their perceived virtues (2:12-20). They conspicuously do "what is right" (*dikaion*: 2:10, 12, 16, 18; 3:1, 10; 4:7, 16; 5:1, 15). They obey the law (*nomos*, 2:12), have knowledge of God (*gnōsin theou*, 2:13), and boast that they are "the Lord's servant" (2:13) and that God is their "Father" (*patera*, 2:16). They are vulnerable to misfortune—they may suffer injustice (3:1-12), childlessness (3:13–4:6), and premature death (4:7-20)—but in the final judgment they will stand before those who cause their suffering with the unquenchable assurance of God's blessing (5:1-5).

Who or what is responsible for sustaining the justice that discriminates between the righteous and wicked? The opening exhortation is addressed to the kings and rulers of the world, the visible sovereigns of political power in everyday life, but it is not they who control the levers of justice. The hidden authority working behind the scene is Wisdom, the spirit of God that permeates the world and examines the hearts and minds of all who profess to "love what is right" (*agapēsate dikaiosunēn*, 1:1). Wisdom makes herself known to those who trust God (1:2). If kings and judges who have power over the multitudes seek Wisdom, they will find her. "She readily appears to those who love her," indeed, "She herself goes about looking for those who are worthy of her" (6:12, 16).

Can Wisdom hold together righteousness and justice, ensuring that all who desire to bring their thinking to maturity will be judged equitably? The sage's answer:

> The real beginning of wisdom is to desire instruction with all your heart. Love for instruction expresses itself in careful reflection. If you love Wisdom, you will keep her laws. If you are attentive to her laws, you can be assured that you will live forever. If you live forever, you will be near to God. If you desire wisdom [*sophia*] with all your heart, you will know what good leadership is. So if you, who take charge over peoples, want to keep enjoying the thrones and symbols of power that you presently possess, honor wisdom [*sophian*] so that you may rule forever. (Wis 6:17-21)

Life and Death; Mortality and Immortality

The contrast between the fates of the righteous and the wicked is embedded in the corollary distinction between life and death, mortality and immortality. The first mention of death occurs in the opening exhortation: "Don't seek death [*thanaton*] through the error of your ways. Don't invite destruction on yourself by what you do" (1:12). The context indicates that the author has in mind the "ungodly" (*asebēs*, 1:16), those who have no reverence for the divinity in life. With twisted reasoning, they claim that no deity gives meaning to life at its beginning, which is a matter of mere chance, not purposeful intention (2:2), and no god judges life's accomplishments or failures at its end. Death is inevitable and final. There is no life after death, and there is no real meaning to life before death. Their philosophy of living a life that does not value anything about life is to seize pleasure wherever it may found, with no regard for costs or consequences.

Come then! Let's enjoy all the good things of life now. Let's enjoy creation to the fullest as we did in our youth. Let's drink our fill of expensive wines and enjoy fine perfumes. Let's pluck every fresh blossom of spring as we pass by. Let's crown ourselves with rosebuds before they wither. Let's make sure that no meadow is left untouched by our high-spirited fun. Let's leave evidence everywhere that we made the most of this life, because this life is all we have. (Wis 2:6-9)

Wisdom's sage refutes this philosophy by arguing that the godless do not know the mysteries of God, the reward of holiness, or the prize for living a virtuous life (2:22). They do not know that life's beginning does have purpose, because God created human beings as "perfect representation[s] of his own unique identity" (2:23b; cf. Gen 1:26-28). They fail to understand that God never intended for death to be only a mechanistic ending to life: "God created everything [*ta panta*] so that it might exist" (1:14). God created humans (*ton anthrōpon*) for "incorruptibility" (*aphtharsia*; CEB: "to live forever"), that is, with the capacity for imperishable existence (2:23). The capacity to "live forever" (*athanatos*, 1:15, literally, "without death") is not a natural or independent quality of human existence; it is a gift from God that enables an enduring relationship with Wisdom and her virtues (7:22-24; see below). Hence the twinned exhortation that frames Part I: seek justice (1:1-15) and seek wisdom (6:1-21).

If all things are made to live and not die, then where does death come from? The sage breaks away from biblical tradition by making two unprecedented assertions: (1) "God didn't make death [*thanaton*]" (1:13; contrast, for example, Deut 32:39; Sir 17:1; 41:4); and (2) "Death [*thanatos*] entered the universe only through the devil's envy" (2:24). There is ambiguity in the sage's understanding of death. Is it death understood as mortality in general that God did not make? Is it physical death as punishment for injustice? Is it the ultimate death of separation from God?[33] The argument seems to be that the general death of mortality applies to all, the righteous and the wicked alike, but the wicked summon death through what they do and say. They consider death "their friend," they "made a treaty with death," they are kindred spirits: "death and the ungodly belong together" (1:16). Nor did God make death as an unavoidable punishment for sin, the sage seems to argue; the punishment of the ungodly is the result of their own conscious decisions to oppress and abuse the righteous (2:10-20; but see 12:10-11 and the discussion below).

The understanding of death the sage seems to have in mind is the ultimate death signified by a total separation from God. In the final judgment, the wicked will disappear "like dust in the wind, like frost that is stripped away and scattered by a mighty wind, like smoke that rises and is immediately dispersed by the wind, like the memory of a stranger who spends the day and then is gone" (5:14). On the day of final accounting, the righteous dead, by contrast, will have an afterlife of fellowship with God. There is no such thing as a tragic death for the godly (4:7-15): "Virtue is what will be remembered, and this means immortality [*athanasia*]" (4:1; cf. 1:15).[34]

What then is Wisdom's connection with life and death, mortality and immortality? Can Wisdom hold together all aspects of life from beginning to middle to end (7:18), however that "end" is to be understood? The sage offers Solomon as the paradigm for reflecting on this question. Solomon begins his speech by reflecting on his limitations, the mortality he shares with all human beings (7:1-6), and "because of this," the sage says, Solomon "called out, and Wisdom's spirit came to me" (7:7). At the end of his reflections, Solomon has learned that "immortality [*athanasia*] is to be found by becoming part of Wisdom's family" (8:17).

The Ethics of Immortality, Human and Divine

The thematic frame that brackets Part I equates seeking justice (1:1-15) with seeking wisdom (6:1-21). The linchpin between the two is introduced at the end of the opening exhortation: "Doing what is right means living forever" (*dikaiosune gar athanatos estin*, 1:15). Immortality (*athanatos*) is linked with ethical behavior (*dikaiosune*). Understood in terms of Wisdom's virtues, the ethics of immortality are manifest in "loving good" (*philagathos*, 7:22; CEB: "overflowing with kindness") and "loving people" (*philanthropos*, 7:22; cf. 1:6; 12:19; CEB: "delighting in humans"). Wisdom, the perfect image of God's moral goodness, permeates creation and enables humans both to participate in divine ethics and to actualize them in daily life (7:24b, 26b).

On the human side of the ethics of immortality, the sage argues that without a correct understanding of one's accountability before God in the final judgment there can only be moral chaos. Unrestricted self-gratification will be life's objective. Such is the default philosophy of the wicked, who see no reason to love either the good or people (1:16–2:24). The sage contrasts their ethic with that of the righteous, who understand virtue and justice to be the only path to fulfillment in this life and to eternal fellowship with God in the afterlife (3:1–5:23).

Solomon's reign exemplifies the corporate and political manifestation of the individual's ethics of immortality. He knows that if "anyone loves to do what is right, laboring with Wisdom will produce every virtue" (8:7). His acquisition of wisdom's virtues brings the assurance that he can govern his kingdom with justice that is as close to God's ideal as possible. These virtues steer both him and the people he rules to potential immortality. Pagan rulers, by contrast, "don't judge rightly" or "keep the Law" or "act according to God's plan," and as a consequence God's judgment falls hard on them (6:4-8). They squander fulfillment in this life and in the afterlife on "bad living" (5:13).

On the divine side of the ethics of immortality, wisdom is the agent through which the whole of creation is refashioned for submission to God's commands (19:6). As the sage has already asserted, "He [God] will arm creation itself for the fight against his foes. . . . The cosmos itself will join with him to defeat those who have wandered from reason" (5:17, 20). From primordial Adam to Moses (10:1-21), Wisdom enacts God's justice by delivering the righteous from the wicked, which the sage understands as a divine ethic aimed at creating "eternal glory" (*doxan aiōnion*, 10:14) for "a holy people and a pure generation" (10:15).

To buttress the argument for Wisdom as God's agent of justice in history, the sage retells the story of Israel's exodus from Egypt as a series of seven contrasts between God's use of creation to punish the Egyptians but bless the Israelites (11:1–19:17):

- the waters of the Nile, "polluted with blood and gore," are a sign of God's judgment against the Egyptians, but the water God provides in the wilderness saves the Israelites (11:1-14);

- a plague of frogs and other small animals torment the Egyptians, but God provides a feast of quails for the Israelites (16:1-4);

- the Egyptians are bitten by locusts and flies and "there was no healing that was able to keep them alive," but the Israelites survive bites from poisonous serpents, "because your mercy traveled along with them and healed them" (16:5-14);

- the Egyptians are hounded by hail, rain, and lightning and realize that "God's judgment . . . was hunting them down," but the Israelites feed on manna that falls from heaven like snow, which is "a minister of your gift, completely nourishing and fulfilling the desire of those in need" (16:15-29);

- darkness engulfs and terrifies the Egyptians, and neither fire nor shining stars nor their own magic provides any illumination, but God provides "an incredible light" for the Israelites, a "fiery pillar to lead them on their way on the unknown journey" (17:1–18:4);

- the Egyptian firstborn are "swept away in judgment," but the Israelites are spared "in order that our fathers might rejoice and put their whole trust in the promises they had been given" (18:5-25);

- and in the climatic event at the Reed Sea, the Egyptians met "a strange death" sent by an angry God who assaulted them "without mercy," but the Israelites found an "open path" to the "amazing wonders" of their saving God (19:1-17).

Two moral principles undergird the sage's account of God's ethics: (1) creation itself is a moral agent for divine justice, disseminating punishment to the ungodly and blessing to the godly; and (2) the reason for blessing is obedience to God; the reason for punishment is willful disobedience to God. Both principles are succinctly stated in 16:24: "Creation, which serves you, the one who made it, tenses itself in preparation for the judgment of those who have done wrong and then relaxes itself again in order to benefit those who have put their trust in you." The sage augments the description of creation tensing and relaxing itself by using a music metaphor that suggests God's objective is to achieve a tonal balance between assonance and dissonance. "If we are careful to observe events," the sage writes, "we can see just how the elements of the universe are transformed. It's the same transformation that happens when someone changes the sounds that a harp makes by changing the key while continuing to play the same melody" (19:18). In short, creation is an orchestra of many instruments and various sounds; God is the composer/conductor who transforms noise into harmony.

Can Wisdom hold together all aspects of the ethics of immortality, both human and divine? When the human side of the equation is askew because the wicked pursue temporal pleasures and mortal rewards at the expense of the just, God's ethics of immortality corrects the injustice with a final judgment that restores the righteous. "Evil can never overcome Wisdom," the sage insists. "She stands strong from one end of the world to the other. She is a marvelous governor over everything in between" (7:30b–8:1).

What of the divine side of the equation? When and if the ethic of immortality, innate in God's transcendence and actualized in Wisdom's immanence, goes askew, who (or what) then is the "marvelous governor" that corrects the imbalance? The sage does not address this question and implies that it should never even be asked. The opening exhortation hints that those who set their mind on God's goodness should not test God's justice with "perverse reasoning" (1:1-3). The sage might well have had Qohelet and Job in mind, the two most vocal voices of dissent in the biblical wisdom tradition.

Affirmations the sage seeks to quarantine from doubt remain nonetheless vulnerable to scrutiny. Even as he insists that God tempers justice with mercy and forbearance that leaves sinners time for repentance (12:2), he acknowledges that for whatever reason God creates some people with a genetic predisposition to evil that leaves them cursed from the day they were born (12:10b-11). Echoing the friends' rebuke of Job for cursing the day God birthed him into a life of pain and suffering "for no reason" (Job 2:3), the sage celebrates God's inscrutable sovereignty: "After all, who will question what you have done? Who will oppose your decision? . . . There's no one to whom you must prove that your judgments are right" (12:12a, 13b; cf. Job 11:11-12). He declares that God loves everything that exists and "hates" nothing that God has created (11:24) but affirms with equal conviction that God "hated" the Canaanites and used Israel to destroy them (12:3, 6). From one event to the next in the sage's retelling of Israel's history, God's universal love for all people (*philanthropos*) privileges a particular people as the chosen recipients of divine blessing. The "others," defined as Israel's enemies, "deserved to be punished and tormented" (16:1; 4, 9), "robbed of light and . . . locked up in darkness" (18:4), and swallowed up in a death that God knew was inevitable (19:4). The sage seeks to insulate such acts from criticism by attributing them to the mysteries of divine justice, through which God called a special people out of the land of Egypt and gave them great honor (19:22; cf. 18:8).

Gentiles may have been linked with Judeophobia in first-century Alexandria, as noted previously, but in the sage's retelling of Israel's history with the Egyptians, the Jews responded with xenophobia of their own.[35] God's hatred for the Canaanite "others" is mirrored in the Jews antipathy toward their Greek and Egyptian "others." They practice the "ritual murder of children," engage in mad orgies of "blood, murder, theft, and deception," corrupt marital bonds and legitimate genealogies with adultery and promiscuity. In sum, "they live in such a way that everything they do is wrong" (14:23-28). For these reasons, the sage concludes, these ethnic others are enemies of God and the Jews. Their lives are worth less than dirt (15:10). They deserve to be punished, tormented, and tortured (16:1-4; cf. 15:23).

The ethics of immortality leads to a positive transformation of ordinary values; this is the sage's primary message. But there remains in Wisdom of Solomon a more mortal, more conventional "common ethic,"[36] attributed both to God and to humans, that conforms to what one might expect in any secular society. The discipline of hope and faith required to unlearn the world and transcend its principles was hard to sustain in

Diasporic Judaism. Hence the need for sages and their quest for wisdom, imperfect as they may be.

For Further Reading

Cheon, S. *The Exodus Story in the Wisdom of Solomon: A Study in Biblical Interpretation.* Sheffield, UK: Sheffield Academic Press, 1997.

Clifford, R. J. *Wisdom.* Collegeville, MN: Liturgical Press, 2013.

Collins, J.J. *Between Athens and Jerusalem: Jewish Identity in the Hellenistic Diaspora.* Second edition. Grand Rapids, MI: William B. Eerdmans, 2000.

Grabbe, L. *Wisdom of Solomon.* Sheffield, UK: Sheffield Academic Press, 1997.

Hengel, M. *Judaism and Hellenism.* 2 vols. Philadelphia: Fortress Press, 1974.

Kolarick, M. *The Ambiguity of Death in the Book of Wisdom 1-6: A Study of Literary Structure and Interpretation.* AnBib127. Rome: Pontifical Biblical Institute, 1991.

Limburgh, J. S. *God, Grace, and Righteousness in Wisdom of Solomon and Paul's Letter to the Romans: Texts in Conversation.* Leiden: Brill, 2013.

Nickelsburg, G. W. E. *Resurrection, Immortality, and Eternal Life in Inter-testamental Judaism.* HTS 26. Cambridge, MA: Harvard University Press, 1972.

Passaro, A., and G. Bella, eds. *The Book of Wisdom in Modern Research: Studies on Tradition, Redaction, and Theology.* Berlin: Walter de Gruyter, 2005.

Perdue, L. G. *The Sword and the Stylus: An Introduction to Wisdom in the Age of the Empires.* Grand Rapids, MI: William B. Eerdmans, 2008.

Reese, J. M. *Hellenistic Influence on the Book of Wisdom and Its Consequences.* Rome: Pontifical Biblical Institute, 1970.

van der Horst, P. W. *Studies in Ancient Judaism and Early Christianity.* Leiden: Brill, 2014.

Xweavits, G. G., and J. Zengellér, eds. *Studies in the Book of Wisdom.* Leiden: Brill, 2010.

Conclusion
The End of Wisdom

If wisdom *begins* with the fear of the Lord (Prov 1:7), then what is its *end?* The question may be considered from two perspectives. First, is there a time when the pursuit of wisdom is finished, when the search for knowledge and understanding comes to an end? Second, what is the end toward which wisdom strives, that is, what are its ultimate goals and objectives?

(1) The answer to the first question may seem self-evident. Surely the horizons of knowledge are constantly expanding; every discovery opens the door to new questions. There is always more to know, never an end to thinking about both the known and the unknown. From this perspective, it seems clear that the pursuit of wisdom is always a journey and not an arrival. There will be intervals when the pace slackens and the fruits of discovery can be savored—and contemplated—but these are inevitably only pauses before curiosity triggers another investigation. On further reflection, however, we recognize that while the thirst for knowledge is without end, it can be stymied or forbidden. Full comprehension of some things seems perpetually or at least persistently beyond our reach. We are limited by our humanness, by the biology of our cognitive capacity, and this of course can be frustrating and sometimes paralyzing. But where knowledge is elusive, imagination is empowering. More difficult to overcome are the forces that would forbid the quest by declaring some knowledge off limits. When punishment is the price to pay for transgressing the boundary between what can and cannot be known, then the pursuit of wisdom becomes dangerous. Such is the "Garden of Eden moment" when one

faces the ethical dilemma posed by forbidden wisdom (Gen 3:1-7): to eat from the tree of the knowledge of good and evil or not to eat; that is the question.[1]

Biblical wisdom affirms that while there is no end to the search for wisdom, there are limitations and boundaries that deny full acquisition of what is sought. The paradox is that the sages considered discernment of the limitations and boundaries of wisdom to be the essence of wisdom itself. Such discernment was not a diminishing punishment for hubris, it was instead an ennobling reward for daring to be fully human. From the sages' perspective, to be human was to live *as if* a God-like transcendence of reality was both possible and endlessly rewarding. One lives into the full expectations that come with being created in the image of God (Gen 1:27) not only by obeying the commandments rooted in the Torah and proclaimed by the prophets, whether those commandments are comprehensible or not, but also by thinking about the incomprehensible with resolve that defies reason. The "fear of the Lord" manifests itself not in a cowering subordination to divine authority that shuts down inquiry but in an invincible curiosity that believes there is more to know and understand about the meaning of life than what the eyes can see.

Proverbs begins the wisdom collection with the affirmation that piety is the first step in acquiring wisdom. Sirach and Wisdom conclude the collection with the same affirmation. Qohelet and Job speak from the center of this literary record a correlate truth with equal conviction: there is more to be learned about the meaning of life than subordination to its limitations. To discern where the boundaries are one must press to the outermost limits of what is humanly possible, at which point imagination enlivens the wait for what remains yet to be discovered.

(2) What are wisdom's ultimate goals and objectives? Proverbs 1:2-7 provides not only an introduction to the book of Proverbs but also a table of contents for the five-book collection surveyed here. Within a span of six verses, this prologue sets forth the essential objectives that those who seek wisdom strive to attain: instruction, insight, shrewdness, knowledge, prudence, learning, and skill. These various goals all have to do with cognitive matters in one way or another. Persons who attain wisdom will

think more deeply, be more discerning, have a keener insight into the complexities and nuances of decision making. At the center of this list are three terms that connect thinking with doing, knowledge with ethics: righteousness, justice, and integrity (1:3; cf. 2:9). The ultimate goal of wisdom, according to the sages' curriculum, is the shaping of a "moral self" attuned to the character of God.[2] Being wise means living ethically. To live ethically, one must be in a constant intellectual pursuit of meaning.

What the sages envision as the reciprocal relationship between wisdom and moral character, Greek philosophers framed as the indivisible linkage between epistemology and ethics. In both cases, seeking wisdom and doing justice are aspirations to divinity. In both cases, indeed, in cross-cultural and transhistorical wisdom traditions throughout the ancient world, aspirations for ultimate achievements must settle for penultimate discoveries. This is of course a limitation, but it is also the harbinger of possibility. Put differently, penultimate discoveries are not possible without seeking wisdom that is ultimately elusive.[3] On this point, Socrates and biblical wisdom speak with one voice: "Let us try to put the truth in this way. In God there is no sort of wrong whatsoever; he is supremely just, and the thing most like him is the man who has become as just as it lies in human nature to be . . . it is the realization of this that is genuine wisdom and goodness, while the failure to realize it is manifest folly and wickedness."[4]

I am tempted to put a period here and end this discussion of wisdom's "end" with an uncontested affirmation of its place in the intellectual economy. In answer to the first question, we had to concede mitigating factors could thwart the quest for wisdom; with the second question there is also an important caveat. The pursuit of wisdom in the ancient world presupposed divinity. Whatever the vagaries of life on earth, the search for meaning was inextricably linked to the understanding that the gods (or God) were the ultimate arbiters of what could be known. An a-theistic wisdom was inconceivable. There were representatives of what we would call "humanistic" thinking in the ancient world, but they were minority voices largely subordinate to religious orthodoxy.

This religious perspective on wisdom held sway in one way or another until the late Middle Ages when humanism regained its footing (e.g., Dante, Giotto, Petrarch) and a renaissance of thinking took hold.[5] Seismic shifts in the marketplace of ideas moved the search for wisdom from Galileo to Darwin, from understanding the world as a "creation" to exploring it as a "cosmos," from conceding the limitations of human capacity to exploiting its evolutionary advancements. Hard science raced past soft science, rendering the metaphysical thinking of theology and philosophy more an obstacle to be overcome than a co-participant in the intellectual quest. Explosions in the fields of chemistry, physics, and biology gave birth to cognitive-based hybrid studies like neurobiology, cognitive science, and neurotheology. Cloud-based cognitive systems, like IBM's "Watson," made unlimited wisdom immediately available to anyone. To a voice command, he/it responds with unbounded confidence: "Together we can outthink anything." Science is the "new wisdom," and the imperatives of technology seem to have surpassed theological reflection on abstract concepts such as the "fear of the Lord."[6]

As noted in the introduction to this book, *Wisdom Literature*, biblical scholars have given little or no attention to ancient Israel's contribution to this larger history of wisdom. In the last two decades, however, scholars working in other fields have begun to construct a meta-discourse of wisdom that presents important questions for all who look to biblical wisdom for guidance. Paul Baltes, a psychologist who explores the relationship between wisdom and religion, frames the issue as follows:

> What is the nature of the relationship between religion and wisdom? I offer two impressions. First, the stronger the role of organized religion in a given society, the more likely it is that wisdom or a related concept will be part of a sophisticated cultural dialogue and agenda. The reverse is likely true as well. As societies evolved, they generated religion as one mental and institutionalized form of spirituality and insight into the human condition. Second, however, I am impressed by another factor. My reading suggests that religions constrain how far wisdom developed. In fact, there may be a point beyond which religion becomes a hindrance to the generalizability or transcultural validity of wisdom. In other words, religions (or other ideologically framed belief systems)

160

are among the fathers of wisdom but also among its limiting "enemies." Religion opens and closes the mindful territory of wisdom.[7]

Stephen Hall condenses Baltes's observation to a sharply framed question: "Does religion ultimately promote, or undermine, human aspirations to wisdom?"[8]

The question grows out of a postmodern skepticism that distrusts all "ideologically framed belief systems," as Baltes puts it, but its seeds are planted in the rich soil of biblical wisdom. The sages who give us Proverbs, Sirach, and Wisdom of Solomon advocate Wisdom (with a capital *W*) that is hospitable to skepticism but not swayed by its doubt. Qohelet and Job speak of a wisdom (with a small *w*) that remains open to divine revelation without being closed to autonomous thinking and discovery. Inside this generative tension lies the *beginning* and *end* of biblical wisdom and an important clue to its abiding contribution to the intellectual economy of the modern world.

Notes

Introduction: Wisdom and *wisdom*

1. S. S. Hall, *Wisdom: From Philosophy to Neuroscience* (New York: Vintage Books, 2010), 34. Biblical scholars also use this distinction, e.g., C. Fontaine, *Smooth Words: Women, Proverbs, and Performances in Biblical Wisdom* (Sheffield, UK: Sheffield Academic, 2002); D. Hankins, *The Book of Job and the Immanent Genesis of Transcendence* (Evanston, IL: Northwestern University Press, 2015), 11–13.

2. The adjective *'ārûm* ("intelligent") is part of the vocabulary of wisdom, although it is used with both negative and positive connotations. The serpent's "wisdom" connotes a negative "cunning" or "scheming." Proverbs frequently uses the same adjective, however, to describe the desirable wisdom of the prudent (e.g., Prov 14:8: "By their wisdom the prudent [*ḥokmat 'ārûm*] understand their way, but the stupidity of fools deceives them." See further, M. V. Fox, *Proverbs 1–9: A New Translation with Introduction and Commentary*, AB18A (New Haven, CT: Yale University Press, 2000), 35–36. On the larger question of the serpent's depiction in ancient Near Eastern literature and in the Old Testament, see J. H. Charlesworth, *The Good and Evil Serpent*, Anchor Bible Reference Library (New Haven, CT: Yale University Press, 2010).

3. R. Wagner and A. Briggs, *The Penultimate Curiosity: How Science Swims in the Slipstream of Ultimate Questions* (Oxford: Oxford University Press, 2016), 25–34, 437.

4. *Timaeus*, 90c, in *Plato: Complete Works*, ed. J. M. Cooper (Indianapolis: Hackett Publishing Company, 1997), 1289.

5. See further, J. Day, "Wisdom and the Garden of Eden," in *Perspectives on Israelite Wisdom: Proceedings of the Oxford Old Testament Seminar*, ed. J. Jarick (London: Bloomsbury T & T Clark, 2016), 336–52.

6. See, for example, Eliphaz's charge that Job speaks with a "clever tongue" (*lĕšôn ʿărûmîm*) that resembles that of the "clever/intelligent" (*ʿārûm*) serpent (Gen 3:1; see note 2 above).

7. For introductions, see D. Jacobson, "Wisdom Language in the Psalms," in *The Oxford Handbook to the Psalms*, ed. William P. Brown (Oxford: Oxford University Press, 2014), 147–60; M. Goff, *4QInstruction* (Atlanta: Society of Biblical Literature, 2013).

8. For overviews and discussion of how scholarship on wisdom literature has evolved, see K. Dell, "Studies of the Didactical Books of the Hebrew Bible/Old Testament," in *Hebrew Bible/Old Testament: The History of Its Interpretation*, ed. M. Sæbø, vol. 3, part 1, The Nineteenth Century (Göttingen: Vandenhoeck & Ruprecht, 2013), 603–24; W. Kynes, "The Nineteenth-Century Beginnings of 'Wisdom Literature,' and Its Twenty-First Century End?" in *Perspectives on Israelite Wisdom*, *Proceedings of the Oxford Old Testament Seminar*, ed. J. Jarick (London: Bloomsbury T & T Clark (2016), 83-108. On whether the conventional genre designation "wisdom literature" has a future, see W. Kynes, "The 'Wisdom Literature' Category: An Obituary," JTS 69 (2018), 1-24; S. Weeks, "Is 'Wisdom Literature' a Useful Category?" in H. Najman, J.-S. Rey, E. J. C. Tigchelar, eds., *Tracing Sapiential Traditions in Ancient Judaism* (JSJSup 174; Leiden: Brill,2016), 3-23; M. Sneed, "Is the 'Wisdom Tradition' a Tradition?" CBQ 73 (2011), 50-71.

9. D. Penchansky, *Understanding Wisdom Literature: Conflict and Dissonance in the Hebrew Text* (Grand Rapids, MI: William B. Eerdmans, 2012), 1–3; idem, "Wisdom" in *The Oxford Encyclopedia of the Bible and Theology*, ed. S. E. Balentine (Oxford: Oxford University Press, 2015), 2:421.

10. See T. Curnow, *Wisdom: A History* (London: Reaktion Books, 2015).

11. E.g., E. Conze, *Buddhist Wisdom: The Diamond Sutra and the Heart Sutra* (New York: Vintage Books, 1958).

12. E.g., M. Bernal, *Black Athena: The Afro Asiatic Roots of Classical Civilization* (London: Free Association Books, 1987); V. Mudimbe, *The Invention of Africa: Gnosis, Philosophy, and Order of Knowledge* (Bloomington: Indiana University Press, 1988); D. Masolo, *African Philosophy in Search of Identity* (Bloomington: Indiana University Press, 1993); T. Obenga, *African Philosophy: The Pharaonic Period, 2780–33 BC* (Dakar, Senegal: Per Ankh, 2004); D. Akoto-Abutiate, *Proverbs and the African Tree of Life: Grafting Proverbs on to the Ghanaian Tree of Life* (Leiden: Brill, 2014); M. Mawere and T. Mubaya, *African Philosophy and Thought Systems: A Search for a Culture and Philosophy of Belief* (Cameroon: Langaa RPCIG, 2016).

13. See, for example, the work of psychologist Paul Baltes, "Wisdom as Orchestration of Mind and Virtue," an unpublished manuscript available on the website of the Max Planck Institute for Human Development, Berlin; http://library.mpib-berlin.mpg.de/ft/pb/PB_Wisdom_2004.pdf (accessed February 3, 2017). The title of the book by Stephen Hall, from which the citation that begins this chapter is taken, is case in point: *Wisdom: From Philosophy to Neuroscience*. See, for example, his discussion "Eight Neural Pillars of Wisdom" (61–210).

1. Proverbs

1. W. Benjamin, "The Story Teller," in *Illuminations*, ed. Hanna Arendt (New York: Schocken,1968), 108.

2. Seventeenth-century English natural philosophy traced its roots to Solomon's proverbial wisdom, which was thought to have been recorded in legendary books, now lost, but preserved by "wise" philosophers such as Plato and Aristotle. See, for example, Francis Bacon's appeal to the "glory of [Solomon's] inquisition of truth" as validation for his advancement of the scientific method (*Advancement of Learning in The Works of Francis Bacon*, vol. 3 (London, 1857–1874;

facsimile reprint, Stuttgart/Bad Cannstatt, 1989), 299, as cited in S. Gaukroger, *Francis Bacon and the Transformation of Early-Modern Philosophy* (Cambridge: Cambridge University Press, 2001), 73; cf. P. Harrison, *The Bible, Protestantism, and the Rise of Natural Science* (Cambridge: Cambridge University Press, 1998, 137–38).

3. For a listing of the parallels between Proverbs 22:17 and 24:22, see M. Fox, *Proverbs 10–31*, Anchor Bible 18b (New Haven, CT: Yale University Press, 2009), 757–60. For an English translation of *Amenemopet*, see M. Lichtheim, *Ancient Egyptian Literature: A Book of Readings*, vol. 2, *The New Kingdom*, 2nd rev. ed. (Berkeley: University of California Press, 2006), 146–63.

4. For other antecedent Egyptian, Mesopotamian, and Syrian texts that have similarities to Proverbs, see M. Fox, *Proverbs 1–9*, Anchor Bible 18a (New Haven, CT: Yale University Press, 2000), 19–23.

5. For an accessible overview, see T. Curnow, *Wisdom: A History* (London: Reaktion Books, 2015).

6. P. Espak, *The God Enki in Sumerian Royal Ideology and Mythology* (Wiesbaden: Harrassowitz, 2015). See further, B. Alster, *The Instructions of Shuruppak* in Mesopotamia: Copenhagen Studies in Assyriology, vol. 10 (Copenhagen: Akademisk Forlag, 1974); B. Alster, "Additional Fragments of the Instructions of Shuruppak," *Aula Orientalis* 5, no. 2 (1987): 199–206. For the Adapa myth, see S. Izre'el, *Adapa and the South Wind: Language Has the Power of Life and Death* (Winona Lake, IN: Eisenbrauns, 2001).

7. "Worldview" is a concept that has its origins in modern philosophy (especially Kant and Hegel) and as such typically involves seeking answers to six basic questions: (1) What is the nature of our world? (2) Where does it (the universe) come from? (3) Where are we going? What is our destiny, fate, or probable outcome? (4) What is good and what is evil? (5) How should we act? (6) How do we acquire knowledge about what is true and what is false? C. Vidal, "What Is a Worldview?" originally published in Dutch as C. Vidal, "Wat is een wereldbeeld? (What is a worldview?)," in *Nieuweheid denken: De wetenscappen en het creatieve aspect van de werkelijkheid*, ed. H. van

Belle and J. van der Veken (Leuven: Acco, 2008), 71–85. English version available at http://cogprints.org/6094/ (accessed January 29, 2016). I am indebted to the essay by Annette Schellenberg for this reference: "Don't Throw the Baby Out with the Bathwater: On the Distinctiveness of the Sapiential Understanding of the World," in *Was There a Wisdom Tradition? New Prospects in Israelite Wisdom Studies*, ed. M. R. Sneed (Atlanta: SBL Press, 2015), 115–43. It is wise to be cautious about applying this modern concept to premodern societies like ancient Sumeria, Egypt, Mesopotamia, and Israel; nonetheless, it is a useful entry into ancient thinking to recognize that there would have been no conceivable answer to any of the questions above that was not entrenched in a presupposition about the primary role of the gods.

8. S. N. Kramer, *The Sumerians: Their History, Culture, and Character* (Chicago: University of Chicago Press, 1963), 116.

9. A sage—nobody rejects his word—

Clever, extra-wise, he [Adapa] was one of the Anunnaki [the gods], . . .

He does the baking with the bakers, . . .

He takes the boat out and does the fishing for Eridu.

S. Daly, "Adapa," in *Myths from Mesopotamia: Creation, the Flood, Gilgamesh, and Others*, rev. ed. (Oxford: Oxford University Press, 2000), 184.

10. One version of the Sumerian tale, *The Death of Gilgamesh*, reports that Gilgamesh received from Ziusudra the rites of Sumer, which he brought back to Uruk in order to restart civilization after the flood:

Having founded many temples of the gods, you [Gilgamesh] reached Zi-ud-sura in his dwelling place. Having brought down to the Land the divine powers of Sumer, which at that time were forgotten forever, the orders and the rituals, he (?) carried out correctly the rites of hand washing and mouth washing.

"The Death of Gilgamesh," in *The Electronic Text Corpus of Sumerian Literature*, by J. A. Black, G. Cunningham, E. Fluckiger-Hawker, E. Robson, and G. Zólyomi, http://www-etcsl.orient.ox.ac.uk/section1 /tr813.htm (accessed February 2, 2016).

11. On "moral reasoning" and ethics in Proverbs, see A. Stewart, *Poetic Ethics in Proverbs: Wisdom Literature and the Shaping of the Moral Self* (Cambridge: Cambridge University Press, 2016).

12. W. McKane, *Proverbs: A New Approach* (Philadelphia: Westminster, 1970), 266; Fox, *Proverbs 1–9*, 37.

13. See further, C. B. Ansberry, *Be Wise, My Son, and Make My Heart Glad: An Exploration of the Courtly Nature of the Book of Proverbs*, BZAW 422 (Berlin: Walter de Gruyter, 2010).

14. Stewart rightly cautions against a rigid binary (either-or) reading of antithetical proverbs, noting that Proverbs contains both "proto-typical" and "non-prototypical" models of wisdom: the wise *typically* prosper but not always; the wicked are *usually* punished, but *there are gaps* in the implementation of moral norms. Even so, as Stewart concedes, even non-prototypical experiences effectively promote the general reliability of the prototype by presenting themselves as outside the norm; see *Poetic Ethics in Proverbs*, 177–80.

15. Fox, *Proverbs 10–31*, 481. Some have sought to construct a meta-narrative from the episodic poetry of Proverbs. See, for example, W. P. Brown's suggestion that Proverbs 1–9 depicts a parent's education of a child, who leaves home to explore the wider world (represented by the proverbial/public wisdom sayings in Prov 10–29), and finally returns as a mature adult who has found the ideal wife (31:10-31; see W. P. Brown, *Wisdom's Wonder: Character, Creation, and Crisis in the Bible's Wisdom Literature* [Grand Rapids, MI: William B. Eerdmans, 2014], 29–66). For a similar effort to discern a thematic unity in Proverbs, see A. Moss, *Proverbs, Readings: A New Biblical Commentary* (Sheffield, UK: Sheffield Phoenix, 2015). Such "narrative" readings, however, diminish the strategic role poetry plays in teaching one how to think imaginatively about the learning process; see, for example, Stewart's critique: "the poetry of Proverbs is not simply a literary form

but is a central means by which the sages teach one how to think, to discern, and to seek wisdom. The sages of Proverbs convey the nature of learning through the medium of poetry. Indeed, the *how* emerges through the images, metaphors, and dynamism of the poetic lines" (Stewart, *Poetic Ethics in Proverbs*, 43, italics original).

16. Cf. Fox's discussion of the Socratic view of ethics in *Proverbs 10–31*: "the sages of Proverbs intellectualized virtue by making it a species of knowledge. Virtue is an act of cognition" (*Proverbs 10–31*, 943).

17. On the "fear of the Lord" as a "temporal priority," that is, piety as the *first* thing to learn, not the *sum total* of learning, see Fox, *Proverbs 1–9*, 67–68.

18. See also the occurrences of the phrase "fear of the Lord" in Proverbs 1:29; 2:5; 8:13; 10:27; 14:26, 27; 15:16, 33; 19:23; 22:4.

19. Plato, *Theaetetus*, 155d; Aristotle, *Metaphysics*, 982b. On imagination as indispensable to the creation of meaning in Proverbs, see Stewart, *Poetic Ethics in Proverbs*, 170–200. On wonder as the dominant motif not only in Proverbs but also in Job and Ecclesiastes, see Brown's seminal study, *Wisdom's Wonder*.

20. An important exception occurs in the prologue and epilogue to Job (1–2 and 42:7-14) and in the divine speeches (38:1–42:6); For discussion of Proverbs' God, see L. Boström, *The God of the Sages: The Portrayal of God in the Book of Proverbs*, Consectanea Biblica: Old Testament Series 29 (Stockholm: Almqvist & Wiksell, 1990).

21. On wisdom as a transcendent force, see also Sirach 24:1-33 and Wisdom 6–19.

22. So multiple Septuagint manuscripts, Aquila, Symmachus, Theodotion, Philo, and the Vulgate.

23. Fox, *Proverbs 1–9*, 294.

24. One measure of the importance of Proverbs 8 in the intellectual history of religious thought is the role it played in the Arian controversies of the early church in the fourth century CE. Arianism held that the

Son of God was created by the Father and therefore was neither coeternal with the Father nor of one substance with the Father. The Council of Nicea (325) judged Arianism to be heresy, thus the opening words of the Nicean creed: "I believe in one God, the Father Almighty, Maker of all things visible and invisible. And in one Lord, Jesus Christ, the Son of God, begotten of the Father, Light of Light, very God of very God, begotten not made, being of one substance with the Father."

25. Literally, "I was delights" (*wā'ehyeh ša'ăšu'îm*). The pronoun "his" is not present in Hebrew, but it is implicit (cf. LXX, "It is I [Wisdom] who was the one in whom he [God] took delight"). CEB's rendering of verse 30b—"I [Wisdom] was having fun"—is more paraphrase than translation and misses the primary thrust of the verse. As Fox puts it, "God, rather than Wisdom, is the one experiencing the delight here" (*Proverbs 1–9*, 287).

26. "The activity of understanding, it seems, is superior in excellence because it is the activity of study, aims at no end apart from itself, and has its own proper pleasure, which increases the activity. . . . Such a life would be superior to the human level. For someone will live it not insofar as he is a human being, but insofar as he has some divine element in him" (*Nichomachean Ethics*, X, 1177b, 20–28 emphasis added; Aristotle, *Nichomachean Ethics*, 2nd ed., trans. T. Irwin [Indianapolis: Hackett Publishing Company, 1999]), 164; cf. *Met.* 982b-28-983a11). On the Socratic nature of Proverbs' epistemology, see M. Fox, "The Epistemology of the Book of Proverbs," *JBL* 126 (2007): 669–84; Fox, *Proverbs 10–31*, 934–45.

2. Job

1. Ancient Near Eastern Job figures are discussed below. In Greek texts, beginning at least as early as Hesiod in the eighth century BCE, Prometheus's struggle against the gods resonates with the biblical Job (cf. S. E. Balentine, *Have You Considered My Servant Job? Understanding the Biblical Archetype of Patience* [Columbia: University of South Carolina Press, 2015], 122–34). On Indian Job figures, see D. J. A. Clines, "In Search of the Indian Job," *VT* 33 (1983): 398–418; M.

Reddy, "Job and His Satan Parallels in Indian Scripture," *ZAW* 91 (1979): 416–22. On Eastern Job figures, see C. W. Edwards, "Greatest of All the People in the East: Venturing East of Uz," *Review and Expositor* 99 (2002): 529–40.

2. Translations and line citations from "Man and His God," trans. S. N. Kramer, *Ancient Near Eastern Texts Relating to the Old Testament*, 3rd ed., ed. J. B. Pritchard (Princeton, NJ: Princeton University Press, 1969), 589–91.

3. Translations and line citations from W. G. Lambert, "The Poem of the Righteous Sufferer, Ludlul Bel Nemiqi," in *Babylonian Wisdom Literature* (Oxford: Clarendon Press, 1960), 21–62. See also the poem from Ugarit, "The Just Sufferer," text translated by M. Nissinen, in *Prophets and Prophecy in the Ancient Near East*, ed. P. Machinist (Atlanta: Society of Biblical Literature, 2003); *Writings from the Ancient World 12* (Atlanta: Society of Biblical Literature, 2003), 184.

4. Lambert, "The Poem of the Righteous Sufferer," 27.

5. Translations and line citations from W. G. Lambert, "The Babylonian Theodicy," in *Babylonian Wisdom Literature*, 63–91.

6. See below, 45–46.

7. "The Adversary" renders the Hebrew word *haśśāṭān*, "the satan," which is the way the expression is written in each of its occurrences in Job (1:6, 7, 8, 9, 12; 2:1, 2, 3, 4, 6, 7). The definite article (*ha*) indicates that the word should be understood as a title that is descriptive of one's function and responsibility. *Haśśāṭān* is one of "the divine beings who came to present themselves before the Lord." He functions as a kind of prosecuting attorney who seeks to establish the facts of a case in the pursuit of justice. He is not God's opponent; his intentions are neither evil nor opposed to God's purposes. Instead, he serves as God's advocate by probing human behavior for truth and faithfulness. His role is to question all meaning that claims to be transparent and inscrutable. In this sense, the Adversary is the epitome of the sage who searches for truth. English translations tend to omit the definite article and capitalize the Hebrew noun as *Satan*, thus inviting

identification with the devil of later Jewish and Christian literature. Although this reading is demonstrably incorrect on critical grounds, it has nevertheless contributed to a major trajectory of interpretation that sees a genetic connection between Job's encounter with *haśśāṭān* and the *diabolos* ("devil," Greek, Latin) who, according to the New Testament, is Jesus's principal adversary (e.g., Matt 4:1-11; Mark 1:12-13; Luke 4:1-13).

8. The Hebrew word translated as "evil" in 2:10 is *rāʿ*. The same word occurs in 1:1, 8, and 2:3. In Hebrew *rāʿ* is the antithesis of *ṭōb* ("good"), hence the frequent use of the expression "good and evil" to denote a comprehensive knowledge enabling humans to make wise and autonomous decisions concerning what is in their best interests, most famously in Genesis 2:16-17: "The LORD commanded the human, . . . don't eat from the tree of the knowledge of good and evil." English translations typically render *rāʿ* as "evil" when the referent is a human being (e.g., CEB in 1:1, 8; 2:3) but as "bad" (or some other equally muted term) when the referent is God (e.g., CEB in 2:10). The obvious intent is to avoid imputing evil to God. In the book of Job, however, the possibility that a good God might indeed be doing evil things to Job is at the core of the story, as in the NJPS translation. For further discussion of the issue from multiple perspectives, see M. Bergmann, M. J. Murray, M. C. Rea, eds., *Divine Evil? The Moral Character of the God of Abraham* (Oxford: Oxford University Press, 2013).

9. The expression "there is no one like him on earth" is normally reserved as a description of God's distinctiveness. It is used with reference to humans only here and in 1 Samuel 10:24 (D. J. A. Clines, *Job 1–20*, WBC 17 [Dallas, TX: Word Books, 1989], 24).

10. On this phrase, see S. E. Balentine, "For No Reason," *Interpretation* 57 (2003): 349–69.

11. I appropriate this way of framing the issue from R. Wagner and A. Briggs, *The Penultimate Curiosity: How Science Swims in the Slipstream of Ultimate Questions* (Oxford: Oxford University Press, 2016). For

their brief discussion of Job, see pp. 359–60, 434. On Qohelet's pen-ultimate discoveries, see below 83, n. 39.

12. C. Newsom, *The Book of Job: A Contest of Moral Imaginations* (Oxford: Oxford University Press, 2003), 79–89.

13. S. E. Balentine, *Job*, Smyth and Helwys Bible Commentary (Macon, GA: Smyth and Helwys, 2006), 79–88.

14. E.g., Laban's question to Jacob, "Why did you leave secretly, deceiving me, and not letting me know?" to which Jacob responds matter-of-factly, because "I was afraid and convinced myself that you would take your daughters away from me" (Gen 31:27, 31).

15. Cf. the wisdom of Silenus, tutor to Dionysus, which he claims has been passed down as eternal truth: "It is best not to be born at all; and next to that it is better to die than to live" (Plutarch, *Moralia*, xxvii).

16. See the discussion of the Hamlet trope on the desire not to be born—"to be or not to be"—in A. Phillips, *Unforbidden Pleasures* (New York: Farrar, Straus and Giroux, 2015), 175–88.

17. Bildad's speech (25:1-6) is unusually short; Zophar's speech appears to be missing altogether.

18. See the discussion of these terms above, 10-11.

19. Most commentators regard the speeches of Elihu (Job 32–37) to be a later insertion, which suggests that God's speeches were originally located immediately after Job 31:40, "Job's words are complete."

20. Newsom, *Book of Job*, 238: "What the author of the book of Job has composed is something of a tour de force."

21. See above, 30.

22. E.g., "In the face of such a blustering deity, who would not be speechless?" (J. L. Crenshaw, *Old Testament Wisdom: An Introduction* [Atlanta: John Knox, 1981], 111; "It is as if God appears in a tie-dyed T-shirt emblazoned with the words, 'Because I'm God, That's Why.' The gist of the stormy answer he blew at Job was fairly summed up

by hell-and-brimstone preacher John Calvin in five words: 'Who are you to ask?'" W. Safire, *The First Dissident: The Book of Job in Today's Politics* [New York: Random House, 1992], 22).

23. The syntax of the verse is difficult and susceptible to different translations, e.g., "A wise person is mightier than a strong one; a knowledgeable person than a powerful one" (CEB). The translation above follows M. Fox, *Proverbs 1–9*, Anchor Bible 18a (New Haven, CT: Yale University Press, 2009), 744.

24. Job 38:3 and 40:7 are the only places in the Old Testament where God says to a human being, "make me know" (*hôdî'ēnî*) what you know. Ordinarily, God is the one who makes something known to others, for example: "Since God has made all this known to you [*hôdia'*], no one is as intelligent [*nābôn*] and wise [*ḥākām*] as you are" (Gen 41:39); "The LORD informed me [*hôdî'anî*] and I knew ['*ēdā'â*]" (Jer 11:18). Isaiah articulates the implausibility of the Joban poet's idea: "Whom did he [God] consult for enlightenment? Who taught him the path of justice and knowledge and explained to him [*yôdî'ennû*] the way of understanding?" (Isa 40:14).

25. Fox, *Proverbs 1–9*, 32.

26. The Hebrew words in Job 40:10 for "honor and esteem" (*hôd wĕhādār*) are a slight variation of the psalmist's wondrous affirmation of the place of human beings in God's world: "You've made them only slightly less than divine, crowning them with glory and grandeur [*kābôd wĕhādar*]" (Ps 8:5; cf. Job 7:17-21).

27. The Hebrew for the "proud" (*gâbōah*) on whom Leviathan looks (41:34a [Heb 41:26a]) is the same word used to describe Job's regal attire: "Adorn yourself with splendor and majesty [*gōbah*]" (40:10).

28. Cf. T. Krüger, "Did Job, Repent?," in *Das Buch Hiob und seine Interpretationen: Beiträge zum Hiob-Symposium auf dem Monte Verità vom 14–19 August 2005*, ed. T. Krüger, et al. (Zurich: Theologischer Verlag, 2007), 217–19; T. Stordalen, "The Canonical Taming of Job (Job 42:1-6)," in *Perspectives on Israelite Wisdom: Proceedings of the Oxford*

Old Testament Seminar, ed. J. Jarick (London: Bloomsbury T & T Clark, 2016), 187–207.

29. Balentine, *Job*, 692–99.

30. S. Jones, "Job 28 and Modern Theories of Knowledge," *Theology Today* 69 (2013): 486–96; S. Jones, *Rumors of Poetry: Job 28 as Poetry*, BZAW 398 (Berlin: Walter de Gruyter, 2009), 27–104, 232–244.

31. Alternatively, Jones suggests Job 28 draws on the imagery of ancient Near Eastern kings who challenge divine-human boundaries in hopes of achieving eternal life, for example Gilgamesh, who fails to obtain immortality but succeeds nonetheless in attaining wisdom (*Rumors of Poetry*, 31–37; "Job 28 and Modern Theories of Knowledge," 487–89).

32. J. L. Crenshaw notes that these four actions—observation, discussion, establishing hypotheses, and analytic assessment—"nicely describe the cognitive analytic process as the poet understood it" (*Education in Israel: Across the Deadening Silence* [New York: Doubleday, 1998], 217).

33. C. Newsom, "Dialogue and Allegorical Hermeneutics in Job 28:28," in *Job 28: Cognition in Context*, ed. E. Van Wolde (Leiden: Brill, 2003), 304. Particularly striking in this regard is Sirach 3:21, where Sirach warns his students against the very kind of investigation that Job 28:27 advocates: "Don't seek out [*dāraš*] things that are too difficult for you, and don't investigate [*hākar*] matters too perplexing for you." See below, 108-109.

34. Newsom, *Book of Job*, 180.

35. On reading the book of Job from front to back and from back to front, see A. Pelham, *Contested Creations in the Book of Job: The-World-as-It-Ought-to-Be and Ought-Not-to-Be* (Leiden: Brill, 2012).

3. Ecclesiastes

1. "All existing things are born for no reason, continue through weakness and die by accident. . . . It is meaningless that we are born; it is

meaningless that we die" (Jean-Paul Sartre, as cited in J. L. Crenshaw, *Qoheleth: The Ironic Wink, Studies on Personalities of the Old Testament* [Columbia: University of South Carolina Press, 2013], 4–5). Numerous studies view Qohelet as a precursor to modern existentialism, particularly as represented in the work of Sartre's contemporary, Albert Camus (1913–60). Among Old Testament commentators, see especially M. V. Fox, *A Time to Tear Down and a Time to Build: A Rereading of Ecclesiastes* (Grand Rapids, MI: William B. Eerdmans, 1999), 8–11. For bibliography and discussion, see E. Christianson, *Ecclesiastes through the Centuries* (Oxford: Wiley-Blackwell, 2007), 84–86.

2. R. B. Y. Scott, *Proverbs, Ecclesiastes,* Anchor Bible 18 (Garden City, NY: Doubleday, 1965), 191. M. Shields offers a similar, more recent assessment: "What is most perplexing about Ecclesiastes is that a text of this sort is incorporated within a collection of writings that speak of a God who reveals and redeems, who chooses people and cares for them—themes *not only* absent from Qoheleth's words but *frequently* irreconcilable with them" (*The End of Wisdom: A Reappraisal of the Historical and Canonical Function of Ecclesiastes* [Winona Lake, IN: Eisenbrauns, 2006], 10 emphasis added).

3. The verb "to see" (*rā'â*) occurs forty-seven times in Ecclesiastes, including twenty-one times in the first-person singular of the perfect state, "I have seen/observed" (*rā'îtî*: 1:14; 2:13, 24; 3:10, 16, 22; 4:4, 15; 5:12, 17; 6:1; 7:15; 8:9, 10, 17; 9:13; 10:5, 7).

4. Ninety-one occurrences represent roughly 41 percent of the 222 verses in Ecclesiastes, a disproportionate frequency for a book its size (cf. Job, forty-two chapters and seventy-three occurrences; Proverbs, thirty-one chapters and seventy-seven occurrences).

5. The root word for "death" occurs in verbal form, "die," seven times (*mût*: 2:16; 3:2, 19; 4:2; 7:17; 9:4, 5). The same root in noun form, "death," occurs four times (*māwet:* 7:1, 26; 8:8; 10:1).

6. J. J. Collins, *Jewish Wisdom in the Hellenistic Age*, OTL (Louisville, KY: Westminster John Knox, 1997), 14. See further S. L. Adams, who compares Qohelet's focus on death with that of the later sage,

Ben Sira (*Wisdom in Transition: Act and Consequence in Second Temple Instruction*, SJSJ 125 [Leiden, Boston: Brill, 2008], 133–41, 204–10].

7. On the description of the "end of possibilities for all humanity" in the final poem (12:1-8), see C. L. Seow, "Qoheleth's Eschatological Poem," *JBL* 118 (1999): 209–34. The citation is found on p. 234.

8. For additional occurrences, see 2:1, 2, 10; 4:16; 10:19. Fox notes that "Qoheleth uses *śimḥâ* in two ways: (1) enjoyment, the sensation or feeling-tone of pleasure, and (2) a pleasure, a means of pleasure: something that is supposed to (but may not) induce enjoyment, such as wine and music. It is sometimes impossible to know precisely which sense applies in a particular occurrence, but the important consideration," Fox argues, is that "*śimḥâh* never means 'happiness' in Qohelet. Indeed, the pleasures called *śimḥah* never even seem to produce happiness in him" (*Time to Tear Down*, 114, 115).

9. W. P. Brown, *Character in Crisis: A Fresh Approach to the Wisdom Literature of the Old Testament* (Grand Rapids, MI: William B. Eerdmans, 1996), 136–40.

10. J. L. Crenshaw, "Nuntii Personarum et Rerum: Qoheleth in Historical Context," *Biblica* 88 (2007): 294–95.

11. W. P. Brown, *Wisdom's Wonder: Character, Creation, and Crisis in the Bible's Wisdom Literature* (Grand Rapids, MI: William B. Eerdmans, 2014), 159–83.

12. On the ethics of joy, see, C. L. Seow, *Ecclesiastes*, Anchor Bible 18c (New York: Doubleday, 1997), 54–60 and especially the commentary on Eccl 5:8–6:9 (Heb. 5:7–6:9), 6:10–7:14, and 9:1-10; E. P. Lee, *The Vitality of Enjoyment in Qoheleth's Theological Rhetoric*, BZAW 353 (Berlin: Walter de Gruyter, 2005); M. R. Sneed, *The Politics of Pessimism in Ecclesiastes: A New Social-Science Perspective* (Atlanta: Society of Biblical Literature, 2012), 224–28.

13. The number of occurrences of *'ĕlōhîm* ("God," forty times) and *hebel* ("pointless," thirty-eight times) are nearly equivalent. The equivalence may be a statistical coincidence. Alternatively, it may be interpreted

positively, a subtle rhetorical indicator that the power of God is equal to or greater than the power of pointlessness (Sneed, *Politics of Pessimism in Ecclesiastes*, 155, 165–68), or negatively, as a subtle indication of the opposite: *hebel's* claim on life is the near-equal of God's.

14. Seow, *Ecclesiastes*, 199.

15. Crenshaw, "Qoheleth in Historical Context," 298. Cf. D. Hankins's translation of 'ōlām in 3:11 as "infinity" (CEB: "eternity"): "yet he [God] placed infinity in their minds so that humans cannot but fail to find the deed that God has done from the beginning to the end" ("The Internal Infinite: Deleuze, Subjectivity, and Moral Agency in Ecclesiastes," *JSOT* 40 [2015]: 47). See further the discussion of this verse in the last section of the chapter, "The End of the Matter," 79-84.

16. Prov 1:7, 29; 2:5; 8:13; 9:10; 10:27; 14:26, 27; 15:16, 33; 16:16; 19:23; 22:4; 23:7; cf. Job 28:28; Ps 111:10; Sir 1:14, 16, 18, 20, 27; 19:20; 21:11.

17. Cf. Fox, *Time to Tear Down*, 49.

18. M. Hengel, *Judaism and Hellenism: Studies in Their Encounter in Palestine during the Early Hellenistic Period*, vol. 1 (Philadelphia: Fortress, 1974), 43.

19. V. A. Tcherikover, ed., *Corpus papyrorum judaicarum*, 3 vols. (Cambridge, MA: Harvard University Press, 1971–80), as cited in Sneed, *Politics of Pessimism in Ecclesiastes*, 108.

20. Translation by S. Lombardo and K. Bell in *Plato, Complete Works*, ed. J. M. Cooper (Indianapolis: Hackett Publishing, 1997). All subsequent translations from Plato's works are from this edition.

21. For the argument that the overall structure of Ecclesiastes reflects the lines of an ancient Greek public speech, see J. Jarick, "The Rhetorical Structure of Ecclesiastes," in *Perspectives on Israelite Wisdom: Proceedings of the Oxford Old Testament Seminar*, ed. J. Jarick (London: Bloomsbury T & T Clark, 2016), 208–31.

22. On the form and structure of the diatribe, see R. Braun, *Kohelet und die Frühhellenistische Popularphilosophie*, BZAW 130 (Berlin: Walter de Gruyter, 1973), 153–55; cf. T. Krüger, *Qoheleth: A Commentary*, Hermeneia (Minneapolis, MN: Fortress, 2004), 12–14.

23. Translation and line numbers follow E. O'Neil, ed., *Teles [The Cynic Teacher]* (Missoula, MT: Scholars Press, 1977), 35, 49, 51.

24. For references to "I see," see above, n3. "I know" (*yāda'tî*): 1:17; 2:14; 3:12, 14.

25. On the language of the heart in Qohelet, see J. L. Koosed, *(Per)mutations of Qoheleth: Reading the Body in the Book*, LHBOTS 49 (New York: T & T Clark, 2006), 46–52.

26. For the description of Qohelet's contradictions as "Yes/but sayings" (*Zwar/Aber Aussage*), see K. Galling, "Der Prediger," in *Die fünf Megilloth*, 2nd ed., ed. E. Wurthwein, K. Galling, and O. Plöger, HAT 18 (Tübingen: Mohr, 1969), 73–125.

27. "Epicurus," in *Diogenes Laertius, Lives of Eminent Philosophers*, vol. 2, LCL (Cambridge, MA: Harvard University Press, 1931), 655 (X. 128-29).

28. Ibid, 657 (X. 132).

29. Cf. Seow, *Ecclesiastes*, 57.

30. Cf. T. Curnow, *Wisdom in the Ancient World* (London: Bloomsbury, 2010); T Curnow, *The Oracles of the Ancient World: A Comprehensive Guide* (London: Duckworth, 2004).

31. "The Complaints of Khakheperre-Sonb," in M. Lichtheim, *Ancient Egyptian: A Book of Readings*, vol. 1, *The Old and Middle Kingdoms* (Berkeley: University of California Press, 1973, 2006), 147–48.

32. W.G. Lambert, *Babylonian Wisdom Literature* (Oxford: Clarendon Press, 1960). 63-91. Parenthetical line references are from this edition.

33. Ibid., 109, lines 11, 13.

34. Ibid., 149, lines 81-82. For a more extensive discussion of these and other ancient Near Eastern wisdom texts reminiscent of Ecclesiastes, see Seow, *Ecclesiastes*, 60–65.

35. Compare a similar joining of wisdom to obedience to divine commandments in Sirach (e.g., 1:26-30).

36. See above, n 13.

37. Note, however, Qohelet's occasional use of proverbs in isolation (1:14) and in a series (7:1-13; 10:1-20).

38. Fox, *Time to Tear Down*, 81; cf. M. Fox, "The Inner Structure of Qoheleth's Thought," in *Qoheleth in the Context of Wisdom*, ed. A. Schoors (Leuven: Leuven University Press, 1998), 225–38; J. L. Crenshaw, "Qoheleth's Understanding of Intellectual Inquiry," in *Qoheleth in the Context of Wisdom*, 205–24.

39. Fox, *Time to Tear Down*, 96. Compare the following counsel from Sirach:

    Don't seek out things

    that are too difficult for you,

    and don't investigate matters too perplexing for you. . . .

    Think about what

    you have been commanded,

    because you have no need

    for matters that are hidden.

    Don't meddle in things

    beyond your own affairs

    since you have already been shown things

    beyond human understanding (Sir 3:21-23; cf. Wis 1:2).

40. On Ecclesiastes 3:11 in relation to ultimate curiosities and penultimate discoveries, see R. Wagner and A. Briggs, *The Penultimate Curiosity: How Science Swims in the Slipstream of Ultimate Questions* (Oxford: Oxford University Press, 2016), 361–62. Wagner and Briggs note that Galileo quotes Eccl 3:11 as a scriptural validation of his own intellectual quests, which played a major role in the scientific revolution of the seventeenth century. In Galileo's words:

> [one] must not, in my opinion, contradict this statement [Eccl 3:11] and block the freedom of philosophizing about the things of the world and of nature, as if they had already been discovered and disclosed with certainty. Nor should it be considered rash to be dissatisfied with opinions which are almost universally accepted; nor should people become indignant if in a dispute about natural phenomena someone disagrees with the opinion they favor, especially in regard to problems which have been controversial for thousands of years among very great philosophers, such as the sun's rest and the heaven's motion. ("Letter to the Grand Duchess Christina," in *The Essential Galileo*, ed. and trans. M. A. Finocchiaro [Indianapolis: Hackett Publishing Company, 2008], 120–21)

Galileo's investigation of "the sun's rest and the heaven's motion" resonates with Qohelet's desire to know if there was anything more to be learned "under the sun" (e.g., 1:9) or "under heaven" (1:13) about the meaning of life.

41. Crenshaw, *Qoheleth: The Ironic Wink*, 96–97.

42. See above, 15–16.

4. Sirach

1. Ben Sira refers here for the first time in extant texts to the tripartite division of Hebrew scripture, Torah Prophets, and Writings. The ambiguous reference to "other writings" (2) and "the rest of the scrolls" (25) indicates that the compilation of the third part of the collection, Writings, had not yet been finalized (cf. Luke 24:44 with Matt 22:40; Luke 16:16; Acts 13:15).

2. Sirach was originally written in Hebrew, as the prologue makes clear, but only about two-thirds of the Hebrew text is extant in portions of chapters from Qumran and various Geniza fragments.

3. P. Skehan and A. A. Di Lella, *The Wisdom of Ben Sira*, Anchor Bible 39 (New York: Doubleday, 1987), 40. See further in the same volume the section titled "Ben Sira and the Other Books of the Old Testament" (40–45).

4. J. L. Crenshaw, "The Book of Sirach: Introduction, Commentary, and Reflections," in *The New Interpreter's Bible*, vol. 5 (Nashville: Abingdon, 1997), 621.

5. The inclusion of Enoch in the list of ancestors is curious and perhaps signals Sirach's interest in supernatural revelation; see further, B. Wright, "I Enoch and Ben Sira: Wisdom and Apocalypticism in Relationship," in *The Early Enoch Literature*, ed. J. Collins (Leiden: Brill, 2007), 159–76.

6. For these and other examples, see J. T. Sanders, *Ben Sira and Demotic Wisdom* (Chico, CA: Scholars Press, 1983), 29–38. While noting such substantive parallels between Sirach and Theogonis, however, Sanders also effectively refutes T. Middendorp's argument that there are more than one hundred examples of such parallels (*Die Stellung Jesu Ben Sira zwischen Judentum und Hellenismus* [London: Brill, 1973]).

7. Sanders, *Ben Sira and Demotic Wisdom*, 61–63. For the translation of the text, see, M. Lichtheim, *Ancient Egyptian Literature: The Old and Middle Kingdoms*, vol. 1 (Berkeley: University of California Press, 1973), 185–92).

8. Sanders, *Ben Sira and Demotic Wisdom*, 69–101. For the translation of "Papyrus Insinger," see M. Lichtheim, *Ancient Egyptian Literature: The Late Period*, vol. 3 (Berkeley: University of California Press, 1980), 184–217.

9. Skehan and Di Lella compare the lack of unity and coherence in the book to a final editing of a teacher's class notes compiled over a lifetime of teaching (*Wisdom of Ben Sira*, 10).

10. W. Roth, "The Gnomic-Discursive Wisdom of Jesus ben Sirach," *Semeia* 17 (1980): 35–79; J. Collins, *Jewish Wisdom in the Hellenistic Age* (Louisville, KY: Westminster John Knox, 1997), 45.

11. B. G. Wright, "Fear the Lord and Honor the Priest: Ben Sira as Defender of the Jerusalem Priesthood," in *The Book of Ben Sira in Modern Research: Proceedings of the First International Ben Sira Conference, 28–31 July 1996, Soesterberg, Netherlands*, BZAW 255 (Berlin: Walter de Gruyter, 1997), 195–96; cf. S. Olyan, "Ben Sira's Relationship to the Priests," *HTR* 80 (1987): 281–86.

12. On the Seleucid economy and administrative practices, see C. G. Aperghis, *The Seleukid Economy: The Finances and Financial Administration of the Seleukid Empire* (Cambridge: Cambridge University Press, 2004); R. Pirngruber, *The Economy of Late Achaemenid and Seleucid Babylonia* (Cambridge: Cambridge University Press, 2017).

13. J. T. Sanders, "Ben Sira's Ethics of Caution," *HUCA* 50 (1979): 73–106.

14. Collins, *Jewish Wisdom*, 32.

15. The words *musar bōšet*, "instruction in shame," occurs in one of the surviving Hebrew fragments (MS B) as both the title of the poem and in the opening line of 41:14a. The Greek manuscript omits these words.

16. On Ben Sira's efforts to secure the religious and cultural heritage of the Jews against assimilation, see M. Martella, *Foreign Nations in the Wisdom of Ben Sira: A Jewish Sage between Opposition and Assimilation*, Deuterocanonical and Cognate Literature Studies 13 (Berlin: Walter de Gruyter, 2012).

17. The Greek verb "pour out" is the same in 1:9b and 1:10a. The two occurrences may be read as a poetic parallel that indicates equivalence (God's allotment of wisdom to all people is the same as the allotment to those who love God) or as parallelism in which the second occurrence intensifies the first (God "pours" out wisdom on all but "lavishes" wisdom on others). The second option is consonant with Ben

Sira's views on Wisdom's particular presence in Jerusalem (24:8-12; see further, G. S. Goering, *Wisdom's Root Revealed: Ben Sira and the Election of Israel*, JSJSup 139 [Leiden: Brill, 2009], 21–24).

18. Cf. 1 En 42:1-2, which reports that Wisdom could not find a home anywhere on earth, thus accenting Wisdom's hiddenness, not its availability:

Wisdom could not find a place in which she could dwell;

but a place was found (for her) in the heavens.

Then Wisdom went out to dwell with the children of the people,

but she found no dwelling place.

(So) Wisdom returned to her place

and settled permanently among the angels.

19. The apocryphal book of Baruch, which comes from a slightly later period (ca. 167 BCE), clearly makes this equation: "She [Wisdom] is the scroll containing God's commandments, the Law that exists forever" (4:1). See further, G. T. Sheppard, *Wisdom as a Hermeneutical Construct: A Study in the Sapientializing of the Old Testament*, BZAW 151 (Berlin: Walter de Gruyter, 1980), 62–68.

20. Goering, *Wisdom's Root Revealed*, 3–9; cf. S. L. Adams, *Wisdom in Transition: Act and Consequence in Second Temple Instructions*, JSJSup 125 (Leiden: Brill, 2008), 198–204.

21. Crenshaw, "The Book of Sirach," 758.

22. Reading with Greek manuscripts that use the word *phobon*, "fear." Other Greek manuscripts have the word *opthalmon*, "eye," literally, God "puts his eye on their hearts" (Skehan and Di Lella, *Wisdom of Ben Sira*, 279).

23. Cf. C. Camp's observation that by writing himself into the role played by Woman Wisdom in Proverbs 8, Ben Sira becomes "Wisdom Man," which she interprets as an intentionally masculinized personification

that is consonant with Ben Sira's negative attitude toward women (*Ben Sira and the Men Who Handle Books: Gender and the Rise of Canon-Consciousness* [Sheffield, UK: Sheffield Phoenix Press, 2013], 157–72).

24. See discussion above in the section "Form, Structure, and Rhetorical Strategy."

25. A Hebrew manuscript from Masada reads differently—"all things are maintained [*nišmār*] for every need"—but another Hebrew manuscript (MS B, ca. twelfth century BCE) reads "obey" (*nišmā'*), which agrees with the Greek.

26. Stobaeus 1.25, as cited in A. A. Long and D. N. Sedley, *The Hellenistic Philosophers*, vol. 1 (Cambridge, MA: Harvard University Press, 1987), 273. Parallels also occur in Jewish texts roughly contemporaneous with Ben Sira, e.g., *Testaments of the Twelve Patriarchs* and *Testament of Asher* (see further, S. Matitila, "Ben Sira and the Stoics: A Reexamination of the Evidence," *JBL* 119 [2000]: 481–83).

27. In response to the serpent's question, "The woman *saw* [*tēre'*] that the tree was beautiful with delicious food and that the tree would provide *wisdom* [*lĕhaśkkîl*], so she took some of its fruit and ate it, and also gave some to her husband, who was with her, and he ate it" (Gen 3:6 emphasis added). Personal observation—the woman "saw"—is the first step toward attaining wisdom (*śākal*). The Genesis narrative has a negative evaluation of the attainment of wisdom by sensory perception and cognitive insight ("Then they both *saw clearly* and they *knew*," 3:7 emphasis added). Ben Sira agrees: "Sin began with a woman, and because of her all of us die" (Sir 25:24). "Original wisdom" was the "original sin."

28. For discussion of this form of questioning as a means of addressing the issue of theodicy, see P. C. Beentjes, "Theodicy in Wisdom of Ben Sira," in *Theodicy in the World of the Bible*, ed. A. Laato and J. C. de Moor (Leiden: Brill, 2003), 509–24.

29. Cf. Wis 1:2-3: "Those who don't put the Lord to the test will find him. He makes himself known to those who trust him. Perverse reasoning

separates people from God. His power exposes the foolish people who test him."

30. See the discussion above, 110–11.

31. The use of lists or *onomastica* of geographical, cosmological, meteorological, and other natural phenomena is common in ancient Near Eastern literature and often employed in the Old Testament (Job 28; 36:27–37:13; 38:4–39:30; 40:15–41:26; Ps 148; Wis 7:17-20, 22-23; 14:25-26; Skehan and Di Lella, *Wisdom of Ben Sira*, 29). For the characterization of these lists as "scientific," see G. von Rad, "Job XXXVIII and Ancient Egyptian Wisdom," in *The Problem of the Hexateuch and Other Essays* (New York: McGraw Hill, 1966), 285.

32. Skehan and Di Lella, *Wisdom of Ben Sira*, 495.

33. The Elihu speeches (Job 32–37) are a later addition to the book of Job, likely dating to the late Persian or early Hellenistic period. See the discussion above, 28–29.

34. See above, 45–46.

35. For what follows, see the seminal discussion in C. Newsom, *The Book of Job: A Contest of Moral Imagination* (Oxford: Oxford University Press, 2003), 223–33, especially 226–28, 232–33.

5. Wisdom of Solomon

1. J. M. Modrzejewski, *The Jews of Egypt: From Ramses II to Emperor Hadrian* (Princeton, NJ: Princeton University Press, 1995), 73.

2. The gymnasium is often associated primarily with athletic training, but it was also an important locus for education. From the fifth century on, three gymnasia were built in Athens, for example, each one associated with a major school of philosophy: the Academy, Platonism; the Lyceum, Aristotelianism; and the Cynosarges, Cynicism.

3. Modrzejewski, *Jews of Egypt*, 82.

4. The date of the so-called *Letter to Aristeas* and many of the details in its account of the production of the Septuagint are widely regarded as more fiction than fact, but there is little doubt the text encouraged Jewish adaptation to Greek culture. For a seminal discussion, see S. Jellicoe, "The Occasion and Purpose of the Letter of Aristeas: A Re-examination," *NTS* 12 (1966): 144–50. On the larger issue of the Septuagint's role in the religion and politics of the Ptolemaic era, see J. J. Collins, *Between Athens and Jerusalem: Jewish Identity in the Hellenistic Diaspora*, 2nd ed. (Grand Rapids, MI: William B. Eerdmans, 2000), 97–103.

5. Josephus, *Ag. Ap.* 2.65.

6. For an overview of these and other Gentile perceptions of Judaism, see Collins, *Between Athens and Jerusalem*, 6–13

7. Josephus, *Ag. Ap.* 2.92–96.

8. Josephus, *Ag. Ap.* 2.148.

9. P. Schäfer, *Judeophobia: Attitudes toward the Jews in the Ancient World* (Cambridge, MA: Harvard University Press, 1997).

10. *In Flaccum*, 65–71, as translated in Schäfer, *Judeophobia*, 140–41.

11. E.g., D. Winston, *The Wisdom of Solomon*, Anchor Bible 43 (New York: Doubleday, 1979), 20–25; L. G. Perdue, *The Sword and the Stylus: An Introduction to Wisdom in the Age of the Empires* (Grand Rapids, MI: William B. Eerdmans, 2008), 310–13.

12. For the citations from *Prospecticus* B 21 and B 110, see I. Düring, *Aristotle's Protrepticus: An Attempt at Reconstruction* (Göteborg: Acta Universitatis Gothoburgenesis, 1961), 56–57, 92–93. For discussion of the similarities with Wisdom, see J. M. Reese, *Hellenistic Influence on the Book of Wisdom and Its Consequences* (Rome: Pontifical Biblical Institute, 1970), 117–21.

13. Perdue, *Sword and the Stylus*, 325.

14. Plato: *Phaedo* 69C; *Republic* IV, 428a–430e; *Laws* I, 631b-e; Stoicism: Zeno, SVF 3.3.255; 256–261; Philo: LA 1.71–72. For the texts from Stoic writers such as Zeno, see H. von Armin, ed., *Stoicorum Veterum Fragmenta*, vols. 1-4 (Leipzig: Teubner, 1905; reprint Leipzig: K. G. Saur, 2004) [SVF].

15. See further, Winston, *Wisdom*, 117; J. Collins, *Jewish Wisdom in the Hellenistic Age*, OTL (Louisville, KY: Westminster John Knox, 1997), 194.

16. For Aristotle's discussion of Pythagorean cosmology, see *Metaphysica*, I, 5, 986–87; cf. Plato, *Republic*, VII, 12, 530d. See further, D. Winston, "The Sage as Mystic in the Wisdom of Solomon," in *The Sage in Israel and the Ancient Near East*, ed. J. G. Gammie and L. G. Perdue (Winona Lake, IN: Eisenbrauns, 1990), 383–97.

17. The division of cultic worship into two or three types was common in Hellenistic commentary. *The Letter of Aristeas* 134–41 (second century BCE) contrasts the idol worship of the Greeks with the animal worship of the Egyptians; Philo distinguishes among nature worship, idolatry, and animal worship (*On the Decalogue*, 52; *On the Special Laws*, 1:13); the Stoics distinguished among mythical, philosophical, and legislative types of worship (M. Kolarick, "The Book of Wisdom," in *The New Interpreter's Bible*, vol. 5 [Nashville: Abingdon, 1997], 545).

18. Winston, *Wisdom*, 249.

19. On Solomon as the "ideal king," see M. McGlynn, "Solomon, Wisdom, and the Philosopher King," in *Studies in the Book of Wisdom*, ed. G. G. Xweavits and J. Zengellér (Leiden: Brill, 2010), 61–81.

20. Winston, *Wisdom*, 34.

21. J. S. Kloppenborg, "Isis and Sophia in the Book of Wisdom," *HTR* 75 (1982): 76.

22. Eana 307, 24; cited in Kloppenborg, "Isis and Sophia," 75.

23. *Medinet Madi* 3.7-11; cited in Kloppenborg, "Isis and Sophia," 76.

24. L. Grabbe describes Wisdom 11–19 as an example of "Hellenistic Jewish midrash" in which the author draws on Jewish tradition to interpret a canonical biblical text from a context shaped by Greek literature and rhetoric (*Wisdom of Solomon* [Sheffield, UK: Sheffield Academic Press, 1997], 39–43).

25. Collins, *Jewish Wisdom*, 204.

26. Kolarick, "The Book of Wisdom," 440–41; for a list of biblical texts appropriated in Wisdom, see C. Larcher, *Études sur le Livre de la Sagesse* (Paris: Gabalda, 1969), 85–103.

27. J. J. Collins, "The Reinterpretation of Apocalyptic Traditions in the Wisdom of Solomon," in *The Book of Wisdom in Modern Research: Studies on Tradition, Redaction, and Theology*, ed. A. Passaro and G. Bellia (Berlin: Walter de Gruyter, 2005), 144–55.

28. Collins, *Between Athens and Jerusalem*, 186–209.

29. Ibid., 189; Perdue, *Sword and the Stylus*, 302; Larcher, *Ètudes*, 136–37.

30. Adapted from Winston, *Wisdom*, 59–63.

31. Perdue, *Sword and the Stylus*, 319.

32. H. A. Wolfson, *Philo*, 2 vols. (Cambridge, MA: Harvard University Press, 1947), 2, 447, cited in Collins, *Jewish Wisdom*, 231.

33. M. Kolarick, *The Ambiguity of Death in the Book of Wisdom 1–6: A Study of Literary Structure and Interpretation*, AnBib 127 (Rome: Pontifical Biblical Institute, 1991), 156–70; Kolarick, "The Book of Wisdom," 455–56.

34. The noun "immortality" (*athanasia*) occurs in Wisdom 3:4; 4:1; 8:13, 17; 15:3. The adjective "immortal" occurs in Wisdom 1:15 as a descriptor of righteousness. In 4:1 and 8:13, immortality is associated with memory; in 3:4, with the hope of the righteous; in 8:17, with Wisdom; in 15:3, with God's sovereignty. Wisdom of Solomon does

not associate "immortality" or "immortal" with the physical body in the sense of resurrection.

35. See, for example, Perdue, *Sword and the Stylus*, 313–20.

36. Collins, *Jewish Wisdom*, 191.

Conclusion

1. See above, "Introduction," 12-13.

2. See the discussion of the "moral self" in Stewart's discussion: *Poetic Ethics in Proverbs: Wisdom Literature and the Shaping of the Moral Self* (Cambridge: Cambridge University Press, 2015).

3. On curiosity about *ultimate* matters as the root of all *penultimate* discoveries—in both religion and science—see R. Wagner and A Briggs, *Penultimate Curiosity: How Science Swims in the Slipstream of Ultimate Questions* (Oxford: Oxford University Press, 2016), 411, et passim.

4. *Thaetetus*, 176c, in *Plato: Complete Works*, ed. J. M. Cooper (Indianapolis: Hackett Publishing Company, 1997) 176.

5. For a seminal study, see E. F. Rice, *The Renaissance Idea of Wisdom* (Cambridge, MA: Harvard University Press, 1958).

6. Cf. P. Harrison, *The Territories of Science and Religion* (Chicago: University of Chicago Press, 2015), 179.

7. Baltes, "Wisdom as Orchestration of Mind and Virtue," an unpublished manuscript available on the website of the Max Planck Institute for Human Development, Berlin; http://library.mpib-berlin.mpg.de /pb/PE_Wisdom_2004.pdf (accessed February 3, 2017), 70.

8. S. S. Hall, *Wisdom: From Philosophy to Neuroscience* (New York: Viking Books, 2010) 35.

CPSIA information can be obtained
at www.ICGtesting.com
Printed in the USA
BVHW081123050920
588050BV00005B/277